PRAISE FOR
McMillan Rur

"Greg is smart, very smart. The patience and positivity that Greg has when it comes to mapping athletes' careers and the steps to take in between goals is incredible. I think the sign of a great coach is someone who knows how to coach the mind as well as the body and this is where Greg stands out. He's guided me through all the ups and downs that running has thrown at me and helped me to be not only a better athlete but also a better person. "

- Andrew Lemoncello, Olympian

"I attribute most of my success in running to Greg's training philosophy. His way of targeting different training zones at specific times in the training schedule made all the difference for me. He is extremely knowledgeable and a true motivator. Working with Greg, I successfully participated in many world championship and Olympic Trials events. I was able to go from a 2:48 marathon runner to 2:32, winning two marathon titles and having a lot of fun in the process! The plans work."

-Kelly Liljeblad, Houston Marathon Champion

"I have the utmost respect for Greg and am impressed with his abilities as a coach. He understands the principles and philosophies of the great coaches like Arthur Lydiard and is able to relate them to today's runner. I love how this book explains the need for adaptation in a training program as it is so very essential to creating confidence in an athlete."

- Rod Dixon, Olympic Medalist, NYC Marathon Champion

World's Greatest Running Lessons

50 Lessons to Elevate Your Running

Greg McMillan, M.S.

Allison Goldstein

CONTENTS

INTRODUCTION
The Six Pillars of Performance

RUN TRAINING PART 1
First Lessons

RUN TRAINING PART 2
Next Lessons

PREHAB TRAINING
No More Injuries!

FORM TRAINING
Move Better

NUTRITION TRAINING
Feed the Machine

BRAIN TRAINING
It's 100% Mental

TRAINING'S DONE
Ready to Race

McMillan Training Plans

Glossary

This one's for you mom!

Love, Greg

INTRODUCTION
The Six Pillars of Performance

Which runner showed up today?

This is the most important question I've been asking athletes—and teaching them to ask themselves—over the last several years. The answer impacts everything: what type of run they do, how they do it, or if they even run at all that day. The result is that the injury rate in my runners has dropped over 80%. That's right, runners are now five times less likely to get injured using the McMillan training system because of this one specific question. And as we all know, staying injury free is half the battle in enjoying a lifelong running career and racing fast.

This question does more than keep you injury free, however. It enables you to optimize your training, meaning that you get the most from every training session and avoid overtraining. "Bad" workouts disappear, and you finish each run knowing you did exactly what you should have that day. This is not the same thing as just "following the training plan." The training plan assumes you feel "normal" each run . . . but you don't, do you?

Sometimes you feel good. Sometimes you feel bad. It's your ability to tweak the training on a day-to-day basis that will get you to the starting line ready to truly race well.

Just like "Which runner showed up today?" is not standard "running advice," this book is not meant as a typical "training guide." Sure, we'll use a few running plans as examples or starting points, but if you want to learn how to build a training plan or technically structure workouts to reach peak fitness, my book *YOU (Only Faster)* will give you that.

What this book is meant to do is to augment whatever training plan you have chosen. I will tell you everything I tell any of my athletes, from the first-timers to the elites—lessons that are time-proven and simple to use, but very, very powerful.

The lessons address the six pillars of performance:

1. Run Training,
2. Prehab Training,
3. Form Training,
4. Nutrition Training,

5.   Brain Training, and

6.   Racing.

The 50 lessons that follow are organized by pillar so you can jump straight into a topic where you have burning questions (e.g., what should I eat to train my best?), or you can build your knowledge pillar by pillar as you read the book from start to finish. Then, armed with this knowledge and an integrated program like the McMillan system (or whatever training program you choose), you will excel in your run training, stay injury free, improve your running form, fuel for performance, develop a resilient mindset, and race to your highest potential.

At the end of the day, this book is for those of us who would love to have our own personal running coach at our side, telling us exactly what to do (and what not to do). My goal, by the end of this book, is for you to be your own best running coach. You'll be armed with all the practical knowledge I can squeeze into these pages to help you train consistently and effectively and race at your best.

So, as I say to my athletes, let's get going!

RUN TRAINING PART 1

First Lessons

Running is a great teacher. Nothing else has taught me so much about myself or provided so many important lessons that help me not just in running but in life. Whether you are brand new to the sport or a seasoned veteran, here are the top lessons that will help you train smarter, run faster with fewer injuries, and stay active for a lifetime.

Lesson #1: Your Running Routine

When you first start running, it's all about routine. Just like many New Year's resolutions, it's easy to put in a week or two of a new routine, but it's far different to set up a routine that can last past the "twenty-one days to build a habit" phase. Therefore, for my beginning runners, I just want them to find a running regimen that is sustainable (and I care less about how far or fast they run).

I personally like to work with one, three, six, and twelve months as progressive milestones for new runners. First, let's find a routine that can work for a month as you get going. Then, let's refine the routine if necessary so we get to three months of consistent training. From there, we'll work toward six months and then twelve. I know the fitness will come, so again, I worry less about number of miles or speed and more about just maintaining the routine.

If I've done my job correctly, a few things happen:

1. You never have an injury that takes you out of running,

2. You fall in love with the sport,

3. You learn how to adjust training to flow with your life,

4. You start to believe that you can do things you never thought possible, and

5. You're motivated to explore your potential and challenge yourself.

The process comes down to a few key ingredients:

First, you must have a routine that is sustainable and fits within your (everchanging) life schedule. I much prefer a runner to start with a routine that is doable when "life happens" rather than choose a routine that only works when everything is running smoothly. Why? Because life will get in the way. It always does.

And because many runners feel bad if they miss runs, I'd rather have a schedule that will be successful in the tough weeks and onto which we can add training if things are going better. Then, any addition seems like a bonus.

Shirley's a good example. She's an executive at a bank with a demanding job and decided to start running for stress relief and to get healthy (and, I later learned, to also beat the half-marathon time of her younger sister, Linda). Did I mention she is a Type A competitive person?

My biggest challenge was getting Shirley to train less than her sister, who had a less stressful job and more time to train and recover. Linda, who has been running for nearly ten years, runs five to six days per week, so naturally Shirley felt she should do the same, but I knew that would be a mistake. Her life schedule just wouldn't handle it, and since she's Type A, I knew she would feel like she failed if she missed a planned run (highly likely given her job).

After a bit of negotiation, she started with three to four days per week and could add a fifth if the week was going well. This worked perfectly. Shirley felt like she was getting in "extra" training when she got in five days of running and never felt like she missed a run when she ran three days. And best of all, the schedule was sustainable. We breezed through one month, cruised through three months, and now have our sights set on her first half-marathon (with, you guessed it, the time goal of "Anything faster than my sister!").

The bottom line: Pick a routine that is very doable even when your weekly life schedule isn't perfect. It's much better to train in a sustainable way than to try to force a routine that will likely fail. Your routine should be such that it can "go with the flow" of your life. And, importantly, be disciplined about getting in your runs, but remain open to adjusting your routine when you need to. That's a key to lifelong running.

Another lesson is that really bad weeks will happen. Your routine may get compromised, and that's okay; just don't let a few missed runs completely derail you. Ease back into your routine, and again, go with the flow. All is not lost. This happens to every runner. In fact, you'll probably observe some seasonality and ebbs and flows with your running.

For me, for example, I train very consistently in the summer, because I run early in the morning (so there's more light in the summer), and I like it hot. I know, however, that I'll need to use running buddies and other strategies to keep me on schedule through the winter when it's colder and dark in the mornings. You may find this as you train across the year as well.

Speaking of running buddies, the next ingredient for a successful running routine is a training partner. Most of us enjoy solitary runs as a way to think through our lives and regain some mental or emotional balance, but for long-term success, having a training partner, a running group, or something that creates accountability is really, really important.

The "loneliness of the long-distance runner" isn't accurate. I like my solo runs, but I know from experience that if you can find a group or some training partners to meet up with for a few runs, you are more likely to maintain your routine. And today, it's even easier! With so many running groups and online training clubs, adding accountability to keep you consistent is right at hand.

Another thing that can help keep your routine on track is having a big, scary goal. My wife is this way. She likes running, but for her to be consistent, she needs a big goal. Recently, she felt she needed a boost in motivation to maintain her routine, so she signed up for a 30-kilometer trail run. Having run a road marathon before, this distance was definitely doable for her, but running 30 kilometers over trails was also scary enough that she got more disciplined in her running routine. Experienced runners like her often relearn this lesson and must spice up their training with new race distances, race types, and workouts; otherwise their running routine can become a rut.

The key takeaway is that maintaining a routine is an ongoing process, but the most successful runners are the ones that keep getting out the door, allow their routine to flow with life, and develop strategies for accountability, especially when their motivation is low.

Lesson #2: The Most Important Training Lesson

Shortly after I start working with a new runner, I teach the most important training lesson. This lesson is so important, because it will serve you well not just when you start running but throughout your running career. If you always follow it, you'll kick the running injury bug and discover just how good you can be.

When a person starts running, there are a lot of adaptations that take place. New runners notice that, as the weeks go by, their breathing gets more and more under control. Their heart rate is lower (both during exercise and at rest), and they begin to feel more coordinated when they run. Most importantly, their brain no longer screams to stop. The new runner actually begins to enjoy not just running, but running a bit farther and faster.

Here is when the most important training lesson comes in. While your cardiovascular, neurological, and mental systems adapt very quickly to running, the musculoskeletal system (the muscles, tendons, ligaments, bones, and fascia) adapts much more slowly. This is so important that I'm going to state it again: The musculoskeletal system adapts more slowly than the other systems, so even when you feel great and want to advance your training, you must take it slowly to allow the body to get strong enough to handle the running.

This slower adaptation rate is why runners tend to get hurt within three to six months of starting to run. It's also why runners who are coming back from taking time off or an injury often progress too quickly and get hurt. They feel good! They have the cardiovascular fitness and a cooperative brain to run more, but their musculoskeletal system simply can't handle it.

A key role of a coach is to restrain runners from building up the training load too fast. My experience is that it takes the musculoskeletal system 25–50% longer to adapt than the other systems of the body. That's why coaches tell you to listen to your body and why they are always holding athletes back. You simply must be more patient and allow the musculoskeletal system to grow stronger. It will. It just takes a bit more time than most of us would like.

As mentioned, this lesson isn't just for new runners. Experienced runners get injured as well, and it's due to the same issue: The musculoskeletal system needs more recovery time than we often give it. I see this with experienced runners not only when returning from injury or a planned break, but also when they are trying to advance their training load, or even when they are in the midst of their race-specific phase of training. They ramp up the training too fast. The body gets tight. Then come the aches and pains. Then comes the injury.

The bottom line is that the musculoskeletal system is the governor of how quickly you can advance your training. Keep it happy and you will be able to train week after week after week. And, as I'll discuss in a moment, that week-on-week consistency is one of the most important aspects of becoming the best runner you can be.

Here's a recent example of how I used this lesson to benefit a talented new runner. Julie, age 36 and a mom of two little ones, was a new runner who developed quickly. She was a natural, and from the first few weeks, she got fitter faster than the others in my training group. She quickly got comfortable with

25–30 miles per week and was itching to do more. I, too, was excited to see her reach her potential, but I knew we had better be careful.

From experience, I had a feeling she would do really, really well at 40–50 miles per week. She was that talented and driven. But instead of just letting her go from no running to 50 miles per week in three to four months, I deliberately slowed her buildup. Using the knowledge that the musculoskeletal system takes 25–50% longer to adapt, we very slowly eased up to 40–50 miles.

After using eight weeks to build up and get her comfortable at 25–30 miles per week, she wanted to run 25–30 miles one week, then 30–35 the next, then 40–45, then 40–50. You probably agree that that would be too much too soon.

Instead, here's what we did starting in week 9:

Week #	Mileage
9	25-30
10	30-35
11	25-30

12	30-35
13	30-35
14	25-30
15	35-40
16	35-40
17	25-30
18	40-45
19	40-45
20	30-35
21	40-45
22	45-50
23	30-35

As you can see, the buildup was very gradual and always included a "down week" (more on those later) every third week, to give her musculoskeletal system time to adapt.

Julie wasn't thrilled with this plan and really wanted to run more, but I knew if we did it right, she'd avoid the trap so many of us fall into, where she'd get excited about running and then get hurt. Luckily, she's very coachable and stuck to the plan. The result? She never got hurt. She stacked week after week after week of successful running, and here we are, six months from starting the program, and she's ready to tackle her next running ambition: qualifying for the Boston Marathon.

Lesson #3: Consistency Is King

Lesson #3 is another one that is crucial for new and experienced runners alike.

As I mentioned in the last lesson, some adaptations to running come quickly, but most of the adaptations that lead to ultimate success in the sport are long-term. They take quite a while to develop, because you are building a new you.

When you train, you trigger your genes to adapt to the demands of running. Over time, the genes build a new body that is better able to run. In essence, you replace a slower you with a faster you. Keep training, and you replace the faster you with an even faster you.

A good example is how your body adapts to deliver more oxygen to the working muscles. Initially (and pretty quickly), the body responds to consistent running by adding more red blood cells, which carry the oxygen in the blood, and the heart ejects more blood with each beat. But the adaptation that makes a huge difference in oxygen delivery are the capillary beds.

Capillary beds are tiny arteries where the oxygen moves from the blood to the muscle cells. Your frequent running triggers your genes to build more and more capillaries around your muscle cells. You can think of it as more plumbing surrounding the muscle cells, so more blood and oxygen can envelope and enter the working muscle. This is the new you and results in lots more oxygen getting to your muscles. The trick is that it takes months and months of training for the body to build these new structures.

In addition to needing stimulation over time, some of the adaptations your body makes are related to the frequency of the stimulation. The more frequently you are stimulating the body, the more stimulus you provide for the adaptations. As a result, consistent training is a big, big key to becoming the best runner you can be. Simply stacking successful week on top of successful week creates a new and better you. Do this for a few years, and you can become a completely different runner than you are today.

That's why I'm all about the streak of consistent training. I care less about one big training week or one great workout and more about stringing together multiple weeks of training. That's how you'll come by your best running. Yes, you can train hard for a bit and get fast, but the most successful runners who enjoy a long and gratifying career are just really, really consistent.

A good mantra is, "I'm going to train today so I can train tomorrow, I'm going to train this week so I can train next week, and I'm going to train this month so I can train next month." Sure, you will have your recovery periods at the end of your racing seasons, but for the most part, you just keep getting in one successful week after another.

The take-home message is that consistency is our goal. Never put yourself in risky training situations for weeks on end. Instead, think long-term, because life is better when you're running, so let's focus on consistency.

Lesson #4: Obey Your Stress/Rest Cycle

Early on in my coaching career, I was taught this equation by my first coaching mentor, Guy Avery:

Optimal Stress + Optimal Rest = Optimal Progress

Basically, this is the translation: Training and racing reduce your energy stores and causes wear and tear on your body. Rest and recovery help you to repair the damage and restock your energy. However, if that's all that happened, we would never get any fitter, and we would never make any progress. Luckily our body is smart: After a session where we push our limits, we experience a period of "supercompensation" during which our body builds a greater reserve of the "stuff" we need (red blood cells and capillaries—remember those?) in order to be ready for the same stress next time. This can only happen during recovery periods, however, which is why recovery is so important: Without it, we would never improve at all!

Stress + Rest = Progress is a simple principle, and yet too many runners (and quite honestly, coaches, too) focus exclusively on the "stress" part of the equation—the workouts, the mileage, the races—and neglect the "rest" component—easy running, cross-training, days off, sleep, nutrition, and even general relaxation. When runners "under-rest" after hard training and racing, they stunt their fitness progress: Either they fail to fully "supercompensate," or worse, they wind up injured.

In order to advance your fitness to its highest level, you must balance both the stress *and* the rest. The greater the training or racing stress, the more recovery you will require. (And note that recovery could be cross-training, a day off, or a short easy run depending on the runner). That said, the necessary amounts of stress and rest differ runner to runner. Plus, to make matters more challenging, the stress/rest cycle is a continually moving target; countless factors can affect either part of the equation.

I'll use my friend Peter as an example of how important recovery rate is. Peter is a good runner who tends to be better with endurance-oriented workouts and excels at races like the half-marathon and marathon. For years, his training plan included speed work on Tuesdays, a tempo run on Thursdays, and a weekly long run on Sundays. This training rhythm served him well for many years, but once he turned 45, he began to notice that his tempo runs, workouts he normally was very good at, were hit or miss. He'd have a good tempo run one week, then a poor one the next week. Now, given that he is more of an endurance-type runner, you'd predict that his tempo runs would be where he would shine; if he had trouble with any workout, one would expect it to be his speed training on Tuesdays. Not the case.

What was happening was that as he aged, it was taking him longer and longer to *recover* from the speed work on Tuesday. This delayed recovery was leaving him tired for his tried-and-true tempo run. Once we added an extra recovery day between the two workouts (even skipping the speed workout some weeks), his tempo runs once again became a great strength for him, and he went on to set a new marathon personal best (or PR, "personal record") at the age of 48.

The lesson is that we all recover from different workouts at different rates, and those recovery rates may change throughout your running career. As such, you should set up your training based on your unique recovery rate. It's likely that after a workout that is your strength, you'll only require a short recovery, whereas after a workout that is your weakness, you will need extra recovery days. This is important information as you customize your training plan.

As I'll mention over and over, I believe that recovery rates are more important than the training calendar—a challenge for us in today's world where the calendar drives our daily lives and, consequently, our training. It can be challenging, but try your best to be open to adjusting your training when your body and mind require it. The result will be consistently good workouts and a greater chance at success when you toe the line at your next race.

Here's another illustration: Let's say you do an easy run every Friday. On one Friday you feel good, so the training stress is minimal. Yet on another Friday you feel terrible, so the training stress is much greater for that exact same "easy" run. After the former run, you may be able to do a hard workout the very next day. After the latter run, you may need another day to recover, *even though you ran the same or slower pace, for the same distance!*

As this illustration hopefully shows, balancing the stress/rest cycle is really a dance between your planned stress (or rest) and how you actually feel. You need to continually measure the level of stress you *want* from the run against the level for stress you *get* from the run and use that evaluation to inform the "rest" part of the equation. (And yes, a good coach would help you do that—provided you were giving him or her honest feedback. I help my athletes adjust their training all the time based on health/weather/life factors. That's why this lesson is so important!)

In order to maintain an appropriate stress/rest balance, you first have to recognize factors that contribute to stress. Here are some of the more common ones related to running:

- Intensity of run/workout
- Duration of run/workout
- Preparedness for run/workout: fuel, hydration, mental state, physical (musculoskeletal) readiness

I should note that "stress" is not just training stress. Stress is stress, whether it comes from your run, your job, your family, or even a bad night's sleep, and you only have so much stress you can tolerate before you need recovery. Here are some common non-running sources of stress, which range from where and when you do your run to other seemingly "unrelated" life factors:

- Heat
- Humidity
- Wind
- Terrain
- Training partners
- Life/work stress
- Health status

Each of these factors can make your run more or less stressful. Some of them (like being properly hydrated) can be controlled, and some (like the weather) cannot. The point is that the stress of training (and life!) is not just related to what you expect when you look at your training plan; it also has to do with how you feel on the day. You hear the phrase "listen to your body" all the time in running—the concept of obeying the stress/rest cycle is an example of what this phrase is referring to.

In addition to stress, there are many factors that affect your rest, such as:

- Nutrition
- Hydration
- Sleep
- Mental stress
- Environmental stress (e.g., temperature)
- Life stress

These factors all influence how much recovery you get when you "rest." So let's say after a hard tempo workout, you take a day off from running. But you spend that afternoon doing lawn work in 90-degree heat, and then your child gets sick so you're up all night caring for them. Or it's your cross-training day, so you do some light cycling, but you burn the midnight oil studying for a big test, fueling yourself with cookies and soda. How much real rest and recovery are you getting on days like these? Your training plan says you rested, but your body tells you otherwise.

These "life happens" scenarios are why every training plan needs some wiggle room. Returning to a concept we covered earlier, your training plan should be doable on an average week—meaning a week that has typical life stresses cropping up. And this is the real secret to success: You must feel empowered to adjust your training on the fly, meaning you must become your own coach to a certain extent. If there is one concept that has led to so much success in my training system, it's my encouragement of runners to listen to their bodies/minds and make adjustments to balance the stress/rest cycle. It's a very simple practice (or at least it should be), and once you start, you'll see your injuries go away, the quality of each training week go up, and your enthusiasm for training skyrocket. Sounds good, doesn't it?

Quick Recap: Stress/Rest Cycle

Choose a training plan that has wiggle room. In other words, don't pick a plan that requires your life schedule to go perfectly for you to complete your training.

Feel empowered to make adjustments. Too often, runners want to complete every week "to a T," but that's not how it works. Training plans are not set in stone; even the ones I created for Olympians required a lot of adjustments as we actually trained.

Make adjustments quickly and easily on the fly. This is why, in the plans I create for athletes, I provide ranges for things like volume, pace, and number of repetitions. Feeling good? Run the higher volume, the faster pace, and more repetitions. Feeling crummy? Do the opposite.

Err on the side of caution. Runners tend to do too much rather than too little. That's why you hear coaches talk more about holding athletes back in training than pushing them harder.

Balancing the stress/rest cycle doesn't mean you never train hard. That's the first concern runners have when I teach this concept. They think it means they'll never train hard. Wrong. You can train as hard as you like, as long as you give your body the rest it needs so it can adapt and grow stronger and faster.

Lesson #5: The Rule of Too's

People who want instant gratification don't usually stick with running. That's because improvements in running come very gradually, over weeks, months, and even years. Our brains are often in a hurry, but slow and steady is just the way the body likes it.

As we reviewed in earlier lessons, the body is designed to adapt to training, but it takes some time, especially for the musculoskeletal system to adapt. Push your body:

too hard,

too soon, or

too often

and you'll end up over-trained and possibly injured. That's why this training lesson is called the Rule of Too's.

Here's what I teach my athletes so they avoid injury and get a bigger fitness boost from their training:

First, don't fall into the trap of "crash training" (too much too soon). It's a recipe for injury. Instead, be smart and keep your training at a level that your body can adapt to—usually a bit less than what you feel you could actually do.

Second, be careful jumping from one race plan to the next to the next (too hard, too soon, and too often). Runners who don't take at least a little recovery time between race plans often jump into hard workouts too soon, because they get worried that they won't be ready for the next race. A little rest and recovery can go a long way toward preventing injury and burnout.

Third, make sure to schedule "down weeks" in your training plan every third or fourth week (avoiding too hard too often). A *down week* is a week where you reduce your training load (aka mileage) by 15–25% to allow the musculoskeletal system and the mind to recover and rejuvenate for the next training segment. I have found that including down weeks has significantly lowered the injury rate in my runners.

Fourth, to avoid overuse injuries, you must build a more durable body (avoiding too hard). Unlike professional runners, you probably don't have multiple hours per day to devote to "prehab" exercises, so I recommend starting with two to three exercises that target your problem areas (i.e., weak spots or places susceptible to injury), and commit to doing these after every run. (More on this later in the book!)

Now, while athletes with different levels of experience fall prey to different traps, the number one common factor is being in a rush. New runners often see what other more experienced athletes are doing and want to dive right in. However, it's important for these runners to build volume slowly and to be smart about frequency (e.g., if you've never run more than one day a week before, you should gradually progress to two or three days, not jump straight to five). Also, new runners will see the biggest fitness gains the fastest. This is a good thing for motivation, but too much enthusiasm can lead runners to once again do too much too soon. It's crucial that these athletes build their volume, frequency, and intensity slowly over time to allow their bodies to adapt.

Experienced runners, on the other hand, are often in a big hurry to return to full volume and intensity after finishing a goal race. Either they achieved their goal and are excited to continue making fitness gains, or they fell short and are determined to redeem themselves. Either way *there is no rush.*

After a marathon, for instance, you'll retain your base fitness for a while, even if you don't run much; only your race sharpness is lost. (And who cares about that? Your next race is still pretty far away.) Instead of rushing to return to peak fitness, take this time to allow your body to fully heal and for you to recharge mentally.

Another trap experienced runners can fall into, and masters runners in particular, is remembering old times and paces they've run and striving to hit those again (and hit them *now!*). Depending on where you are in your training cycle or how much time has passed since you hit those paces, it's not impossible to do so again, but it is essential to start with slower paces and fewer repetitions and build to faster paces and more reputations over several workouts. *Do not try to hit your goal times straight out of the gate.* Also, especially at the beginning of a training cycle, it is important to spread stressful days farther apart and build in a few more recovery days so your body has more time to adapt.

Remember Julie from Lesson #2? She was talented and eager to train more, but we intentionally controlled her mileage increase so that she never broke the Rule of Too's. This worked for Julie as a new runner, but to be honest, I find it's the secret for oft-injured experienced runners as well. Injuries are a clear sign that you broke the Rule of Too's.

The take-home message is patience. Fitness comes, but only if you are able to keep training.

Coach Q&A: How do I know if I'm overtraining (or under-recovering)?

The following are some signs that you are training too much, too soon, and/or too often:

- Mood—Loss of enthusiasm for several days
- Inability to "loosen up" during runs
- Training performance is consistently better than racing performance
- Resting heart rate is increased by > 5 beats per minute
- Changes in heart rate variability

Coach Q&A: How can I adjust for compromised stress/rest?

There are a number of things you can do to scale back your training and/or bolster your body to get that stress/rest balance back on track:

- Reduce intensity (slow down!)
- Reduce duration (decrease time or number of repeats)
- Spread stress (decrease frequency of workouts, add a rest day)

- Omit stress (skip a workout)
- Focus on caloric density in meals
- Prioritize sleep
- Laughter and quiet time

Lesson #6: Talk Test

At this point, we've talked a bit about monitoring your body's stress level (Lesson #4) and cautioned against too much intensity at the wrong time (Lesson #5). So now let's talk about how to actually gauge your effort, so you know how hard your body is working at a given time. You can use a precise numerical metric like heart rate, but this is not a perfect tool that will work well in all conditions (as I discuss in the next lesson). Instead, what I prefer is a tool that you literally always have with you. It's called the Talk Test: You use your ability to talk to gauge your effort.

We'll get into the specifics of different training zones in the next lesson, but for now, all you need to know is that all workouts fall into four key training zones, which range from the least intense to the most intense. Each zone corresponds to an "amount" you should be able to talk when you're in that zone. As you may suspect, the less intense the run, the more you should be able to talk, and vice versa.

For Endurance Zone workouts—which typically include easy recovery runs as well as the longest runs you'll do—your breathing should be under control, and you should be able to carry on a conversation with your training partner. That's why this has long been called "conversational pace." Sure, you may breathe more heavily going uphill, but for the most part you should be able to chat away.

The Stamina Zone includes "up tempo" efforts that are great at improving your lactate threshold, but they can be finicky workouts: Run too slow and you won't get the maximum benefits, but run too fast and you'll bump into the Speed Zone. Using the Talk Test, Stamina Zone workouts are that perfect in-between where you won't be able to talk for long, but you also shouldn't be huffing and puffing. The Talk Test teaches that you are in the Stamina Zone when you can speak in short sentences like "This pace feels right" or "I think we're going a little too fast right now."

The next zone is the Speed Zone; many runners will complete these workouts on a track. Compared to the previous two zones, this zone involves lots of huffing and puffing, so with the

Talk Test, you can now only speak one or two words during each fast repeat, especially as you get to the last few repetitions. Things like "Too fast" or "Pick it up" are about all you can get out during speed workouts.

By the final training zone, the Sprint Zone, all you can muster are grunts, moans, and the occasional "aack." For most runners, "silence is golden" fits these very fast workouts (which are again often completed on a track); any communication is typically reserved for the recovery time between sprints.

As a coach, I find the Talk Test to be a great way for runners, new and old, to connect with pace, heart rate, and effort. Plus, it's a great tool to use during adverse conditions like when it's hot and humid or windy. In these conditions, it's easy for pace to lag, but that doesn't mean you aren't getting in a good workout. The Talk Test removes the pressure to hit a pace and keeps your training dialed in so you get the most from your workout no matter the conditions.

It's inevitable that as you get further into a workout, you will get more tired. And as you get more tired, it will be harder and harder to adhere to the Talk Test. So what's a runner to do?

Focus on effort.

Just like with pace ranges, there are effort ranges, and as you progress through a workout, you can expect to move from the "less effort" end of the range to the "greater effort" end. For instance, the first two miles of an eight-mile steady state workout will not feel as hard as the last two miles. However, the greatest effort you give in a workout should be comparable to the greatest effort you'd give in a race of the same pace. So in our eight-mile steady state example, let's say the pace is 2:30:00-3:00:00 race pace (meaning the race distance you could complete in 2:30-3:00 hours—marathon pace for faster runners). If this is around your marathon pace, think about how your effort would progress in a marathon. The first part of the workout should feel like the beginning of a marathon, and the second part should feel like later in the marathon: no crazy breathing, but you'll feel very tired. In this scenario, if you start panting, you're in the wrong zone, and you need to back off.

Lesson #7: Zones & Workouts

Running seems like a simple sport, but once a new runner starts hanging around other runners or reading running magazines, she sees that all runs are not the same. That's where the next lesson comes in.

If you're a new runner, you'll eventually start to hear about long runs, tempo runs, speed workouts, strides, hill workouts, and even a very strange-sounding workout, the fartlek. You'll come to learn that experienced runners do different types of workouts at different times and that coaches use all sorts of terms to describe runs.

The bottom line is that over time, coaches and experienced runners have organized runs into groups, or zones, to make a training system. This sounds simple enough, but what gets confusing is that there is no *one* training system; instead, there are almost as many systems of zones and workouts as there are coaches. And to further confuse you, some coaches use the same word to mean two different things!

I'm going to introduce you to the training system I use, which is comprised of four zones. I adopted these zones from scientist Dr. David Martin. His naming system relied on physiology terms, but these seemed meaningless to most runners, so I renamed the zones based on the aspect of fitness the runner would improve by running in that zone: (1) Endurance, (2) Stamina, (3) Speed, and (4) Sprint.

Within each training zone, there are different types of runs and workouts that runners do to help build the desired fitness and get race ready. I'll offer a "crib sheet" here, so that if you're already familiar with these workout terms, you can skip straight to the next lesson. However, if you're new to running and/or prefer a fuller explanation of the zones and workouts, I encourage you to read this lesson in its entirety.

Zones & Workouts "Crib Sheet"

	Zone Workouts	Effort	Talk Test
Endurance Zone	Easy runs Long runs Recovery jogs	Easy to Medium	Carry on a full conversation
Stamina Zone	Steady state runs	Easy-Medium to Medium-	Speak one or two sentences

	Tempo runs Tempo intervals Cruise intervals	Hard	
Speed Zone	Speed intervals Fartlek	Medium-Hard to Very Hard	Speak one or two words
Sprint Zone	Sprint intervals Strides	Hard to Very Hard	Grunts and moans

One quick note before we start our deep dive into the zones and the workouts that fall within them: In what follows, I talk a lot about effort and not so much about paces. That's because I created an online calculator, the McMillan Running Calculator, that makes quick work of getting your exact paces for each type of run. Just visit www.mcmillanrunning.com and you'll quickly see your paces for all runs.

Zone 1: The Endurance Zone

The bulk of a runner's training is within the Endurance Zone. The reason is that the bulk of the energy for running—including racing—comes through the energy systems that are improved with endurance training. Plus, Endurance Zone running gradually builds a stronger and stronger runner's body so you can tolerate more and faster training in the future.

Endurance Zone runs are continuous runs that can last anywhere from 10–15 minutes to several hours. For most runners, these are your regular runs where you go out and just cover distance (or run for time) at your regular "casual run" pace. Your breathing stays under control and you can carry on a conversation when running in the Endurance Zone.

There are three types for runs within the Endurance Zone: easy runs, long runs, and recovery jogs.

Easy Runs

Easy runs are your regular runs just for time or distance. As mentioned above, the effort is easy, and these runs can last anywhere from a few minutes (and may include running and walking) for brand new runners to up to 90 minutes for experienced runners.

Long Runs

After 90 minutes of easy running, coaches traditionally start calling the run a "long run" instead of an "easy run." The reason is that after 90 minutes of easy running, there is a very strong stimulus for the muscles to burn more fat and for the mind to begin experiencing the suffering of fatigue. ("Long run" can also simply mean the longest run in your week, but from a coaching perspective, we're focusing on the physiological effect of the run, which is why we use 90 minutes as the threshold between easy run and long run.)

Long runs start at 90 minutes and, for ultra runners, can last as long as several hours. For most experienced runners, however, the long run is typically between an hour and a half (90 minutes) and two and a half hours, depending on the runner. Performed at least once every 14 days, the long run provides a whole host of important adaptations, which is why you'll see long runs in nearly all training plans.

Recovery Jogs

If long runs are longer, more taxing versions of easy runs, recovery jogs reverse course and are even shorter and slower. Typically, these are used between faster repetitions in speed workouts (often called "recovery intervals") or sometimes even on the day after a very hard and/or long run when you are very, very tired and need a short (10–20-minute), slow run to aid recovery.

Zone 2: The Stamina Zone

The next zone is the Stamina Zone or what some coaches call the "threshold" training zone. As you run faster and faster, you cross a threshold where your body produces more lactic acid than it can remove. Stamina Zone workouts are designed to help push this "lactate threshold" to a faster pace. The lactate threshold pace is such an important predictor of race performance that you'll be hard pressed to find a training plan that doesn't include at least some Stamina Zone workouts.

There are four types of workouts within the Stamina Zone: steady state runs, tempo runs, tempo intervals, and cruise intervals.

Steady State Runs

Steady state runs, also called "sub-threshold runs" because the pace is slightly slower than the lactate threshold, are continuous runs lasting at least 25 minutes and can go as long as 75 minutes. Unlike the Endurance Zone workouts where the effort is easy and your breathing is under control, steady state runs are where things start to change. Your effort rises to easy-medium and your breathing gets a little faster yet still mostly under control.

Many runners haven't performed steady state runs, as the tempo run (detailed below) is the more popular Stamina Zone workout. However, I find the steady state run to be one of the most beneficial types of stamina workouts. While the effort is easy-medium, so the pace isn't too taxing, these are pretty tough efforts because of the duration of running; therefore, be prepared to increase your concentration to stay on pace and to take a recovery day afterwards in order to reap the full benefits. When you incorporate steady state runs into your training, you will notice that suddenly you can run faster with less effort and that your Speed and Sprint Zone workouts (and races) are much faster. It seems that the steady state run greatly enhances the body's ability to use oxygen and remove lactic acid efficiently, and that ability makes faster running easier.

Unlike the three Endurance workouts discussed above, steady state runs are the first workouts that require a warm-up. For this and all the remaining workouts, you should begin the run with 10–20 minutes at an easy pace, which you may follow up with dynamic stretching and faster "strides" (more on these below) before proceeding into the continuous steady state run. See www.mcmillanrunning.com for a video on a proper warm-up.

Tempo Runs

Tempo runs are slightly more intense than steady-state runs and are designed to increase your stamina. As the name suggests, you really improve your running tempo, or "rhythm," with these workouts. Because they are run right at the lactate threshold, they have become the "go to" Stamina Zone workout. I personally find that a runner will see a bigger improvement in her stamina if she does a variety of Stamina Zone workouts (steady state runs, tempo runs, tempo intervals, and cruise intervals), but you'll find many training plans that simply include a weekly tempo run to help boost your stamina.

Tempo runs last between 15 and 30 minutes and are meant to be "comfortably hard," so don't push the pace. Like the steady state run, tempo runs are continuous efforts, but you must preface them with a thorough warm-up.

One note: Some coaches prescribe even longer "tempo runs" (e.g., one-hour tempo), but those are actually steady state runs. Again, terminology can become confusing, but just focus on the duration and intensity of each type of run and you'll perform them perfectly, no matter what the coach calls them.

Tempo Intervals

Tempo intervals are like fast tempo runs broken into repeats with relatively short recovery jogs. They should last between 8 and 15 minutes. Unlike the previous workouts, tempo intervals are the first workouts to allow for a recovery jog (aka recovery interval) between hard efforts. In this case, you jog for 2–5 minutes between each repeat and then start the next one.

For runners who struggle at holding the pace in a steady state or tempo run or who run those workouts too fast, a tempo interval workout can help to teach you how to maintain appropriate stamina effort.

Cruise Intervals

The cruise interval workout was popularized by running coach Jack Daniels. Cruise intervals are essentially shorter and slightly more intense tempo intervals. Like the other Stamina workouts, these are meant to increase your lactate threshold pace. They last 3–8 minutes and, like tempo intervals, are followed by short recovery jogs, although these are even shorter (30 seconds to 2 minutes).

You'll probably find that it's easy to run too fast on cruise intervals. Keeping them under control and working on a smooth, fast rhythm are the keys to improvement here.

Before we move on to the next zone, I want to reiterate that while you can pick one of the Stamina workouts and just repeat it every week or two to boost your lactate threshold, I find that doing the full spectrum of workouts is more fun and ultimately provides a bigger boost to this important threshold. Variety is key!

Zone 3: The Speed Zone

The Speed Zone is where you work on the maximum capacity of your aerobic system, also called your VO_2 max. When experienced runners talk about speed work, this is what they are talking about: repetitions at around your maximum oxygen uptake (aka VO_2 max) pace with short recovery jogs in between.

Repeats in the Speed Zone usually last between 60 seconds and 5 minutes. Because the pace is faster, you must take a recovery jog of about half the distance of the repeat (or jog for the same duration as the faster running). So, if you run a 1200-meter repeat, you would jog for about 600 meters to recover. These workouts enable you to maintain your speed over a longer period of time.

As your fitness improves, you can start to take shorter recovery. Just be cautious of whether your Speed Zone workout is turning into a Stamina Zone workout. (For example, you may hear of experienced runners doing 20–40 times 400-meter repeats with just 100–200 meters jog in between, which would turn the workout into more of a Stamina Zone workout). Both types of workouts are beneficial, of course, but you want to make sure you know the purpose of the workout so that you can make optimal progress toward your specific running goals. A good way to figure out which zone you are in is through the Talk Test (Lesson #6): In the Stamina Zone, where the effort level was medium, you could speak full sentences, whereas in the Speed Zone, the effort progresses to medium-hard and your breathing is elevated to the point where you can really only get out very short sentences or even just single words.

Speed Intervals and Fartleks

While many runners perform speed intervals on a track, running repetitions of specified times for specified distances (e.g., running 400 meters in 90 seconds), you can also do Speed Zone runs by time and effort in what is called a fartlek run. *Fartlek* is a Scandinavian word meaning "speed play," and the originators used fartlek running as a way to get in a speed workout but to do it by effort and without the requirement of a marked track or course.

To help athletes learn effort levels and to provide a break from distance-based workouts, I love to include fartlek runs in my training plans, and I encourage you to use them as well. Here is one example: Start with 10–30 minutes of easy jogging to warm up. Then run 10 repetitions of 1 minute "on" (hard) / 1 minute "off" (easy); this part of the run will last 20 minutes total. For the "on" minutes of the fartlek, you should be running fast enough that you cannot sustain the pace for more than a few minutes. Likewise, the "off" minutes should be run at a very easy jog, so you are ready for the next "on" segment. Finally, jog for 10–30 minutes to cool down.

Zone 4: The Sprint Zone

The final training zone is the Sprint Zone. Workouts in this zone help your top-end speed and consolidate your stride and form. The goal is to run very fast, let the body/mind recover, and then do it again. You get two important adaptations from Sprint Zone training. First, you improve your ability to tolerate and remove lactic acid. Second, you improve your running form. You'll see this in the descriptions of the two Sprint Zone workouts below: sprint intervals and strides.

Sprint Intervals

Sprint intervals (aka lactic acid tolerance workouts) comprise the first Sprint Zone workout. Like the Speed Zone training described above, they are repeated hard efforts with recovery jogs in between. They last only 100–400 meters and are run at about your 0:02:00 to 0:08:00 race pace effort (half-mile to mile race pace for most runners) with very long recovery intervals. It's usually recommended that you take two to five times the duration of the fast running as a recovery jog before starting the next hard effort (or one to two times the distance of the repeat). For example, if you run 200 meters for your hard interval, then you would jog for 200–400 meters before beginning the next one.

The goal of sprint intervals is to flood the muscles with lactic acid and then let them recover. With practice, your leg strength (and mental strength) and ability to buffer lactic acid will improve, allowing you to sprint longer.

Strides

You're probably familiar with "strides," though you may call them wind sprints, pickups, striders or stride outs. They're similar to the fast accelerations that experienced runners do right before a short race. Strides work to improve your sprinting technique by teaching the legs to turn over quickly. However, it's really the neuromuscular system that we're trying to develop here, which is why they last only 10–20 seconds; we don't want lactic acid to build up the way it does during sprint intervals, because lactic acid inhibits the nervous system and interferes with the neuromuscular adaptations that we want.

Accordingly, after each stride, you must jog easily for a minimum of 30 seconds and up to a minute and a half to make sure your muscles are ready for the next one. Skimping on recovery time after each stride is a common mistake. Take advantage of the longer recovery! It will allow you to put more effort into each stride, which really helps develop your speed.

As you might imagine, the pace for strides is very fast—0:01:00 to 0:06:00 race pace (remember, the McMillanRunning.com calculator provides your exact paces for each type of workout).

Note that this is *not* all-out sprinting. The goal of strides is to run fast but always stay under control and focus on excellent running form. You can incorporate some strides during the middle of your run (which many will call "pickups") or at the end. To perform, run fast for 15–20 seconds, and then jog easily for 30 seconds to a minute and a half before beginning the next one. Begin with four strides and build up to ten to twenty. You'll be amazed at how much your finishing kick improves with these workouts.

Summary

Okay. If your eyes are glazing over, that's normal. In fact, you may not care about the zones or workouts, since you'll rely on your training plan or coach to give them to you. However, I wanted to take a moment to walk through the whys and hows of each zone and workout, because they'll be used in examples later in the book, and because this knowledge is useful to tease out which workouts work best for you and which workouts are ideal to prepare you for specific races. (If you're looking for more specifics, I go into this in detail in my book *YOU (Only Faster)*.)

Before moving on, I should note that not all workouts fit nicely into one of the training zones—hill workouts, for example. Plus, many workouts cross multiple zones. This is on purpose, and important, because most races cross multiple zones as well. Therefore, you must practice crossing these zones in training so your body and mind are ready for the demands of the race.

Again, I know that was a lot to swallow, but knowing more about the zones and workouts helps as you look at and execute training plans. You'll have a better idea of how to "read" a training plan, and when you know the purpose of a workout, you'll be better able to adjust it to get the most out of yourself while respecting your stress/rest cycle (like we talked about in Lesson #4!).

Quick Recap: Zones & Workouts

For those who are more data-minded, here is a tabular synopsis of effort, pace, heart rate, and power ranges for the different training zones and the workouts within them.

Effort	Rating of Perceived Exertion (RPE) Scale: 1–10	Talk Test	Race Pace	Heart Rate (% HRR Reserve)	Power (% of rFTPw)	Workouts	
EZ to Med	4–6	Conversation	3:30:00 to 10:00:00	55–78%	80–85%	Easy run Long run Recovery jog	Endurance Zone

65

EZ-Med to Med-Hard	6–8	Sentences	00:25:00 to 2:30:00	75–87%	85–115%	Steady state Tempo run Tempo interval Cruise interval	Stamina Zone

Med-Hard to Very Hard	8-10	Words	00:05:00 to 0:25:00	90-100%	115-125%	Speed interval Fartlek	Speed Zone

Hard to Very Hard	9–10	None	00:01:00 to 0:08:00	90–100%	125–140%	Sprint interval Strides	Sprint Zone

Lesson #8: Variety Avoids Plateau

We've emphasized the idea of consistency—by which we mean continuing to train week after week after week—in earlier lessons, and you just learned about all the different types of training zones and workouts. Yet too often, runners do the *same* training week in and week out. For example, a common pattern followed by experienced runners is to run a speed workout on the track on Tuesday, a tempo run on Thursday, and a long run on the weekend. These runners soon notice that their improvement stalls after a season or two of this training rhythm. The reason is that the body likes variety; you can't keep hammering the same systems over and over again, because eventually they say "I'm done." A new stimulus that targets a different system, however, will force the body to adapt.

Here's one suggestion for someone coming off of a Tuesday/Thursday/Saturday program: Skip those Tuesday track sessions, and instead run hills. What this will do is give your VO_2 max system—which you were stressing with the track sessions—a break, and instead build leg strength and lactic acid tolerance on those hills.

Another alternative is to train for a different race entirely. If you're a serial marathoner, maybe spend a season training for a 10K instead. This will force you to vary the stimulus, because a 10K runner doesn't need to do those super-long steady state weekend runs; instead, you'll probably need to get on the track more often.

You can even do something simple like varying the surface you run on, or even the shoes you wear to run. So long as your body is doing something different, it won't get stale.

The long and short of it is that you can add variety in a number of different ways: within a workout, within a training cycle, or even within a running career. Look at the very top U.S. runners, like Meb Keflezighi, Deena Kastor, Desiree (Desi) Linden, and Shalane Flanagan: They've been successful at running a variety of distances and never really seemed to plateau. If variety is important to them, it should be important to you. Add variety in your training, and you'll find that you can continue to improve.

Lesson #9: Pace Your Fitness Development

Runners are often surprised when I tell them we need to pace their fitness development. They expect that I would want them to get as fit as possible as soon as possible. But that's not the way running works. Fitness is not a perpetual upwards trajectory!

If your goal is to arrive at your goal race in peak physical and mental condition, peaking too soon—meaning that you do too many hard workouts too early, and your body achieves its peak physical condition before your race date—is something we want to avoid. Therefore, the goal of training is actually to control your fitness development and develop certain aspects of fitness before others. This way you can arrive on race day with both your mental and physical abilities at their apex so you're able to perform your best.

Oftentimes, this careful timing means that I'm actually stalling one aspect of a runner's fitness. Usually it's the race-specific training that I delay, because that's the training that will wear you out the most, both physically and mentally. Also, every other type of training is really just preparing you to do your race-specific training, so the more preparation you can fit in, the higher quality your race-specific sessions will be!

Take a marathoner for example: The more speed he or she can build before entering a marathon-specific training cycle, the easier the goal marathon pace will feel. This in turn feeds the runner's confidence, which can make the workouts even better. . . . So it's a self-perpetuating cycle.

If you're still unsure about what it means to "peak" (because that term can be a little vague), think of it this way: A few weeks out from your goal race, you still want to feel a little bit underprepared. If you already feel super prepared, you probably won't be able to sustain that level of physical and mental fitness all the way to the race. You want to be attacking your training, not simply surviving it. Therefore, by being a little "undertrained," you'll feel fresher and more confident come race day.

I learned the importance of pacing fitness development the hard way in high school. My junior year in cross country, I was the top underclassman at the state championship meet. Naturally, I figured I would return the next year and win the whole thing. I continued my training and had a successful spring track season. I then decided to run summer track to get even faster for cross country—and it seemed to work. Not only was I running very fast times in training as we started the cross-country season, but I was winning every meet and even setting some new course records. I was pumped. It was going to happen: I was going to win the state meet.

Then something weird happened. I started to feel a little flat in races; the usual bounce in my step was missing. I lost a big race and just didn't feel "into it" as I was racing. It was weird. As we headed into the championship season, I still won the regional meet, but something was off. I just didn't feel fresh. One part of my brain was excited for the state meet, but another part just wanted it to be over.

Looking back, I was fried. I had extended hard training for too long—from spring track to summer track to a full cross-country season without a real break from race-specific training. I had not timed things well so that I would peak at the final cross-country meet, and that poor planning came back to bite me

At the state meet, I took the lead with 600 meters to go. Normally I have a very, very good kick, and no one passes me in the last 600 meters of a race. That day, however, one runner passed. Then another. Then another. I just didn't have it. I came in fourth.

I was tremendously disappointed as a high school senior, but the experience has helped me immeasurably as a coach. I learned that fitness development and mental development must be meted out across a season and year. You need to plan to be at your peak at just the right time and respect that you can't just keep training the same way for months and months. The body and mind need some cycling up and down of intensity and focus. Train too hard for too long and you'll have the same experience I did.

Instead, respect that you need to pace yourself, literally and figuratively, in training. By adhering to this lesson, you'll arrive at your big race in top condition and be ready to give it your all.

RUN TRAINING PART 2

Next Lessons

The first lessons set the stage for a fun, successful, and long running career. Once you've nailed those, it's time to take your running to the next level.

As I help runners progress, here are the next lessons that result in big performance increases.

Lesson #10: Setting Your Goal

Let's talk about goals. After getting started and completing a few races, new runners start to wonder just how fast they can run. Experienced runners, meanwhile, are always setting goals and looking for improvement. No matter if you're new or experienced, here are the methods I use to help athletes set goals.

Time and Pace Barriers

Once you run a few races, the most common method for setting a goal is to try to break the next time barrier. For example, if a runner runs a 10K in 1 hour and 3 minutes, she often sets breaking 1 hour as her goal. If you look at finish times, particularly in the marathon, you'll see a cluster of runners just under each time barrier: sub 3 hours, sub 4 hours, sub 5 hours, etc. It just seems to be the easiest method for setting a goal when you are close to a nice round number.

However, goal setting doesn't have to be only about overall time. Some runners focus on pace barriers rather than on overall time. Trying to improve from a 9:38/mile pace to a 9:30/mile pace for a half marathon is a good example. Some runners simply care more about pace than overall time, so their goal is to average a certain pace for a race.

No matter if you use a time barrier or a pace barrier, a lot of runners begin their goal setting with this method, and I tend to like it for newer runners. It keeps them focused on improvement, and achieving the nearest time barrier often comes quickly early in their running journey, which builds motivation for the future.

McMillan Calculator Predictions

As you get more experienced (or if you are not close to a time or pace barrier), you start to get more precise in your goal setting. This is because at first, you take big chunks off your personal best, but as you get more experienced, the improvements come in smaller and smaller increments, so goal setting becomes a bit more difficult.

For these runners, the McMillanRunning.com calculator is a great tool to help set realistic yet challenging goals. One key feature of the calculator is that it predicts your race times at other distances. You simply input a recent race and the calculator creates a chart of your equivalent performances at all other distances (assuming you're well trained for that distance, of course).

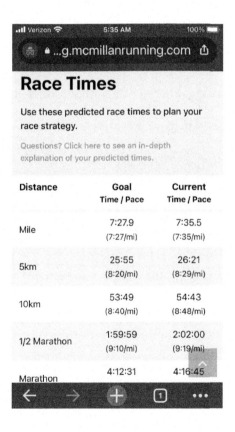

Pretty cool, huh? In one simple tool, you immediately see what you can run right now at other distances in the Current Times column. This is very helpful for setting goals that are coming up soon. For example, if you run a 5K in 26:21 (8:29/mile pace), the calculator predicts a good goal for an upcoming 10K is 54:43 (8:48/mile pace). Having this target pace in mind will help to keep you from starting too fast (most common) or too slow (frustrating after the race) so you get the most from your race. The Current Times feature is particularly valuable for runners who race frequently at various distances, like a summer series of races. Instead of "running blind," you'll have a target pace you can use to help get the most from yourself, particularly in race distances that are less familiar (e.g., 4 miles, 15K).

On the flip side, for runners who are getting ready for a big race in three to four months, the Goal Times feature helps you determine if your future goal is reasonable or not. For instance, if you ran 26:21 for 5K in the summer (from our example above) and decided you wanted to run a half-marathon in the fall, you'd see in the Current Times section that your 5K performance equates to a 2:02:00 half-marathon. Using the earlier time/pace barrier method, you'd probably select sub two hours (1:59:59) as your half-marathon goal. But how do you know if you'll be in that shape by race day? That's where the Goal Times section of the calculator comes in. If you enter your 1:59:59 half-marathon time into the goal input in the calculator, it provides the equivalent performances at all distances. You'll then see that the 5K and 10K predictions are 25:55 and 53:49, respectively. You then know that if you can get your 5K and 10K times down to those predictions in the months leading into your half-marathon, you can probably hit your goal. Since most runners compete in "tune-up" races along the way to their goal race, you would simply sign up for one to three 10K races in advance of your half-marathon and work to get your time down to 53:49. This, along with your goal-pace workouts (discussed below), help you know that your goal is doable.

There is no crystal ball, but the McMillanRunning.com calculator has been used by nearly 20 million runners to help them at least get an idea of what is possible.

Externally Set Times

The last method that runners use is by far the easiest way to set a goal, but often the hardest to know if the goal is doable or not. And that is when the goal is externally set for you.

A great example is the BQ—i.e., the Boston Marathon Qualifying time. To decide who gets to run the Boston Marathon, the Boston Athletic Association, who put on the marathon, set qualifying marks for different age groups and genders. If you want to run the race, you must run faster than your qualifying time to get in. As a result, the goal becomes simple: Hit the BQ time.

The hard part of this process is knowing whether or not that goal is doable. Because the BQ is so important to many runners, I added a Can You BQ? calculator to my McMillanRunning.com calculator to help runners see if the goal is reasonable for them or not.

Anytime a runner faces this type of externally set goal time, I refer them to the McMillanRunning.com calculator a lot. By inputting the goal time, we can easily see what times she needs to hit in other races to match the goal time. Then, it's just a matter of setting up the training (and the racing schedule) to build the fitness she needs. If we've trained right for the goal race and the runner has performed near her predicted times for the tune-up races, then we have a shot. As I'll describe later, it just may take us a few tries to actually hit that externally determined goal time.

Goal-Pace Workout Sequence Tells All

Ultimately, it doesn't really matter how you feel about your goal at the outset, because your training plan should have a sequence of goal-pace workouts that will help you evaluate whether your goal is doable or not.

I started integrating a goal-pace sequence into my training plans many years ago, because runners always wanted to know if they would be able to hit their goal. Of course, no one can see the future, but I knew that if they could hit their goal pace in longer and more challenging goal-pace workouts across the training plan, then we'd get a really good idea of if the goal was achievable or not.

Over a decade or so, I have refined the sequences for each race distance so that each of my plans has just the right goal-pace challenge at just the right time in the plan. What you find is that the first goal-pace workouts, which are short and should be doable, require a bit more effort than you'd like. This is because the body and mind aren't quite used to that pace yet, and you haven't completed the other components of your plan that build your fitness. Then, in the middle of the plan, you really start to nail your goal-pace workouts, and your confidence grows. As you get to the later stages of your plan and the most difficult goal-pace workouts, you find that you now have the physical and, most importantly, mental skills to handle your goal pace.

Runners love this process. When they hit all of the goal-pace workouts in the sequence, they arrive at the race full of confidence and with loads of goal-pace experience. The end result is more often than not a successful day.

On the flip side, the other beauty of the goal-pace sequence is that you can't cheat it. If you can't hit your goal paces in the workouts, then there is no miracle that will happen on race day; you simply need to modify your pacing plan so you can have a successful day. Does this stink? Of course, it does. But it is much more rewarding to have a successful race than to try to run an unreasonable pace and fade miserably.

Plus, running is never a one-time affair. You'll run many races, and it's likely that in future training plans, you will move toward or even surpass your original goal. You may just require one, two, or three training cycles to get there.

Howie had this experience. His dream was to qualify to run the Boston Marathon. He lived in the Boston area, so it was a really important personal goal. The problem was that, based on his two prior marathons and other race equivalents, he was nowhere close to his qualifying time.

I felt we could get there, but it would take time. With his buy-in, we launched a two-year project to get him to his BQ. We used four training cycles across the two years. In the first, we focused on the half-marathon. I felt like it was his sweet spot in performance and would include a nice variety of workouts that would help him not only in the half-marathon but also in his upcoming marathon training. That cycle went well, and he ended up running 1:35:20. The BQ time he needed to achieve for his age group was 3:15:00, which showed a 1:32:39 half-marathon equivalent in the McMillanRunning.com calculator. While his half-marathon was not yet to that level, it was a PR for him and set him up for the next cycle, where we'd run a marathon. I knew this marathon would not be the BQ attempt, but he'd only completed two marathons before, so I wanted him to get more experience with the training and race distance, all with an eye toward our BQ attempt the following year.

This second cycle also went well, and Howie made another step toward his BQ. For the third training cycle, I had him focus on the 10K. He had developed good strength from the half- and full marathon training cycles, but I knew for the BQ, we needed to be a bit faster. Running faster at shorter distances is often a key step to getting faster at longer distances. Fortunately, Howie took to the training and could draw on his well of strength from the half and marathon training. His 10K time now equated to his BQ time. We were definitely getting an idea that the BQ could happen.

The fourth training cycle was all about the BQ attempt. Howie was faster and stronger from the previous cycles and really exceled in training. The result? You guessed it: The coveted BQ. It may have taken a while, but with a smart approach and step-by-step process, Howie built himself into the runner he needed to be to qualify for the Boston Marathon.

The point of Howie's story is that goal setting is fluid. Sometimes you have to take a step back and work on something else (like when Howie worked on his 10K) in order to have a new level of fitness to carry into your goal race plan. Done correctly, many goals—some that even seem really crazy at the time—can become a reality.

Quick Recap: Setting Your Goal

There are three primary ways you can set running goals:

1. **Time and Pace Barriers** – These work well if you're close to a nice round number, like a 3:28:00 marathon

(close to 3:30:00) or an 8:10/mile pace for a 5K (close to 8:00/mile).

2. **McMillan Calculator Predictions** – This tool helps you set a reasonable goal if you have a race coming up soon, and can help you see what benchmarks you need to hit along the way to a longer-term goal.

3. **Externally Set Times** – This is the most cut-and-dried method of goal setting, because there is no wiggle room (e.g., Boston Marathon qualifying times); however, it's also hardest to know if it's realistic.

Lesson #11: Picking the Right Plan

Setting your goal is one thing, but in order to reach it, another part of the equation is picking the right training plan. Here is my checklist for selecting a plan that will work for you:

Be Sustainable and Consistent

Remember this one? I started the book talking about how a sustainable and consistent running routine is a critical lesson in running. When you are selecting your training plan, make sure you consider this. Life rarely goes according to plan, so you need a running plan that has plenty of flexibility (aka wiggle room) built into it in order to accommodate your scheduling needs and how you are feeling.

Let me give you an example. I had an athlete, Trey, start training with me right after he got out of college. He was a collegiate runner, and a good one at that, but now he is an emergency veterinarian. While his life in college was very predictable—run, eat, class, weights, run, eat, sleep—his schedule today is all over the place: He works three overnight shifts when he barely eats or sleeps and then has four days completely off from work.

When he came to me, Trey was very frustrated. He still had big running goals he wanted to accomplish, but he kept failing to stick to his training plan. Sometimes he would get out of work late and have to miss a run. Sometimes he was simply too tired. Plus, even when he did squeeze in his workouts, they were not going well. All of this had him feeling very demotivated—he felt like a failure.

What I had to do for Trey was create a plan for him that would work with his schedule. This meant scaling back a lot from what he had been doing in college, and at first this really upset him. Did I think he was a worse runner today than he had been a year ago? Of course not. But we had to get him on a plan that he could do 100%, no matter what, in order to build back his confidence. This way, when life got in the way, he could still accomplish the training, and whenever conditions were perfect, he could actually do a little more. That's what a flexible plan allows you to do.

When I build training plans—including the one I made for Trey—I make sure they have the following four elements of flexibility:

Flexible Frequency

Make sure your plan has a range for the number of days you'll run per week. For example, I give Trey four to six days of running. On the good weeks, you can run the maximum number of days, and during the challenging weeks, you can run the minimum number of days. Without this flexibility, runners often get demoralized because they can't keep to their schedule and "miss" days of running.

Volume Range

Make sure your plan includes a range for volume each day. (An example from Trey's run this past Friday was a 45–60-minute easy run.) If you're feeling good and have plenty of time, run the higher end of the volume. If you feel tired, stressed, or just off one day, run the lower end of the volume. In this way, you are training optimally for what your body, mind, and life give you on the day.

Pace Range

Make sure you have a pace range to hit and not just one pace. (You'll see the optimal range in the training paces in the McMillanRunning.com calculator.) Because you will feel different from day to day, adhering to a single pace could be overtraining or undertraining based on how you feel. Having a range gives you the flexibility to adjust according to what your body needs.

Recovery-Day Options

Make sure your plan has options for your recovery days (i.e., the days after a hard and/or long workout). This is key, since the bulk of the adaptations occur during the recovery *after* the key training sessions. I provide my athletes with the options to run easy, cross-train, or take the day off. Again, this allows you to train optimally, because you are always adjusting based on how you feel. If you can do this successfully, you'll never get overly fatigued, and the quality of your upcoming training will stay very high.

Stay Injury Free

As has already been mentioned a number of times in this book, it is imperative that you stay injury free. The benefits of running come from consistency, so you need to choose a training plan that will keep you healthy. While it's fun to look at really hard, "scary" workouts, you can't include too many too often in your plan, even if they make sense in theory.

Here's a good example: There is a theory that running on tired legs will help you in the marathon. It conditions the mind and body to the feeling you will have late in the race and stimulates the legs to grow stronger. This is true; *however*, running on tired legs introduces a big risk of injury. Therefore, if you are a runner who gets hurt frequently, then you'll want to avoid this strategy. It's not that the strategy/theory is wrong, it's just that it's wrong for you.

As mentioned before, you also need to make sure your plan has enough recovery in it and is flexible so you can add more recovery if you need it. Older, competitive runners face this issue all the time with training plans. Because many older runners need more recovery, rigid plans that don't allow them to add more recovery if they need it just don't work.

Lastly, make sure your plan includes prehab training. Doing runner-centric core, strength, and mobility exercises is key to warding off injuries so you can race faster and enjoy a lifetime of happy running. I build prehab routines right into my plans, and I'll share some of those routines with you later in the book. However, if you aren't going to use my plans, then make sure the plan you choose includes prehab training.

Capitalize on Your Strengths, Limit Your Weaknesses

Another aspect of choosing the right plan for you is determining if it capitalizes on your strengths and limits your weaknesses. For years, I've taught the idea that not all runners are the same, so not all training plans should be the same either. Yes, there are general training principles, but how they are applied should vary based on the athlete.

Some athletes are naturally better at speed workouts and short races, whereas others are better at longer workouts and long races. This does not mean that athletes with a certain set of strengths can't do races or workouts that aren't their natural fit.

It just means that the training plan should be adjusted so that it works better with their unique traits.

For example, I have race plans for the half-marathon with versions for those who are better at speed (called Speedster plans), those who are equally good at speed and endurance (called Combo plans), and those whom I call "Endurance Monsters." All of the plans will get you ready for the challenges of the race (a half-marathon in our example), but the tweaks I made to each version help that plan to work better for that type of runner. This means that the training will work *with* the runner and not *against* the runner. It's my way of recognizing and appreciating your uniqueness and creating a program that will better fit you. And that always results in better training, which nearly always results in better racing.

Plans on McMillanRunning.com

Naturally, I built all of my training plans to include all of these concepts. On www.mcmillanrunning.com, you'll find plans arranged by your experience level (novice, intermediate, advanced), by your runner type (Speedster, Combo, Endurance

Monster), and by the distance (800 meters to 100 miles) and type of race you're running (e.g., flat > downhill > hilly marathon). I even offer preparatory plans (aka off-season plans like base-building, hills, etc.) so you can improve your capabilities before even starting a race plan. I find that the better prep you do, the better your race-specific training goes. As a result, I built my plans to stack together like LEGOs to build a full training cycle that addresses exactly what you need to get ready to be your best. Have a look at my plans. I think you'll really like what you find.

If you're being honest with yourself and truly listening, your body and mind will tell you if your training plan is serving you well. Chronic tightness, aches, and pains are a sure sign the training load is too much. And if you lose your enthusiasm for training, that's a big red flag. If your running becomes a chore, more often than not your training is too aggressive. Likewise, if you're constantly not hitting your paces in workouts, then you need to adjust.

On the other hand, if you constantly feel like you want to and could run more and you're easily hitting your training paces, then it may be time to step it up. Since most runners are very driven, this scenario is not as common as picking a plan that is too aggressive (which plays no small part in why so many runners get injured). However, it's worth keeping tabs so that if training seems too easy for too long, you'll know to step up your game.

Lesson #12: Which Runner Showed Up Today?

As we covered in the *Lesson #4: Obey Your Stress/Rest Cycle,* how you execute your workout—and in fact, whether you attempt it at all—*should* depend entirely on how you are feeling that day. However, runners often have a tough time trusting how they feel. We want to prove we are tough and follow our plans to the letter!

There are most certainly times when you need to be tough. That said, there are also times to be smart. Differentiating the two is what separates the good runners from the great, and so I'm going to offer you some guidance on using how you feel to manage your training.

Think about the many factors that may affect how you feel on a given day: sleep, nutrition, family stress, work stress, workout fatigue, motivation, mood, hormones, temperature, humidity . . . even the time of day can impact how you feel when you step out the door. That's why, ultimately, *why* you feel a certain way doesn't really matter; it's what you *do* with how you feel that matters.

I feel awful.

Sensations: Your body feels heavy and slow, your movements feel uncoordinated, and your motivation is rock-bottom low.

Advice: Skip the run. Instead, go take a nap or rest, and eat calorically dense comfort food. In this situation, you want to 100% focus on recovery. Don't put a lot of stock in this type of day, meaning don't stress about how missing one run will affect your training. Merely toss it out as the anomaly it is.

I feel okay, but a little tired and sluggish.

Sensations: The pace is not coming easily, your motivation is low, and you just want the run to be done.

Advice: You need to focus on recovery, so run the minimum volume (mileage or time) for the day and run it at the slow end of the pace range. If you have a key workout scheduled, move it, especially if it doesn't play to your strengths (e.g., a steady state run for a Speedster). You're better off attempting it on a day you feel better.

I feel fine. Not great, not bad. Normal.

Sensations: Your usual pace requires the usual effort. You feel appropriately recovered and ready to run.

Advice: Follow your plan! Do whatever is on the schedule, and expect to perform as usual. (And remember, if the workout doesn't play to your strengths, your "usual" performance might be at the slow end of the range—and that's okay!)

I feel good.

Sensations: You're feeling light and fresh, and your usual effort is resulting in a faster pace. You are excited for the run.

Advice: Once again, follow the plan, except now you can expect to run toward faster end of pace range no matter the workout. If there is an option of higher mileage or more reps, do it.

I feel amazing!

Sensations: Your pace is fast despite less effort. You feel light and bouncy, and your legs seem to want to go faster of their own accord.

Advice: On a day like this, you want to take advantage and switch to a key (e.g., goal-pace) workout. Run the maximum volume for the day and aim for the fastest pace (or faster!). However, it's very important to add extra rest and recovery post-workout. You just pushed your body harder than you had planned!

Following your body's cues in this way allows you to be flexible and optimize your training to get the most out of yourself on a given day. It can take some getting used to, especially if you're accustomed to following the letter of the law when it comes to your running plan, but you will benefit in the long run by experiencing fewer negative workouts. That, in turn, will boost your confidence, and it'll become a self-perpetuating cycle that propels you to success.

Quick Recap: Altering Workouts Based on How You Feel

Feeling	Advice
Awful	Don't run, recover
Tired	Run slower/shorter end of range
Normal	Run normal
Good	Run faster/longer end of range
Great	Sub in a key workout!

Coach Q&A: Sometimes I feel terrible when I wake up, but if I run later in the day, I feel fine. How do I know if I'm actually feeling bad or if the feeling will pass?

This type of uncertainty (how do I "really" feel?) is incredibly common. As much as you want to "listen to your body," sometimes it's hard to know what it's saying! For instance, at the peak of marathon training your body is going to be tired all the time, period. Does this mean you need to adjust all your workouts at this stage of training? In a word, no.

A lot of the time, what your body needs is a good warmup. Many runners skip this because they "don't have time" or are anxious to get to the "good stuff." But let me be clear: Warming up (and cooling down) is *part of the workout*. If your body isn't loose and the blood isn't flowing, your best-case scenario is that your first few reps will be slow and stiff. Worst-case, you'll injure yourself. And cooling down is just as important, because it helps get blood flow to fatigued muscles to jump-start recovery so that you can be ready for the *next* workout.

If, after completing the warmup and the first rep (or mile) or two of the workout, you're still feeling as rough as when you started, then you can adjust accordingly. For most of us, it's better to err on the side of caution and "live to run another day."

Lesson #13: The Big Bang Phase of Workouts

Arthur Lydiard, one of my coaching mentors and arguably one of the greatest running coaches of all time, used to have his team run a long run every Sunday. The now-famous Waiatarua course was 22 miles long and included some challenging hills. One of Lydiard's athletes, Murray Halberg (a gold medalist in the 5000 meters), once said that the first 15 miles of that long run were just transportation to get the runner to the last 7 miles where the real benefit from the run happened. This has always stuck with me and informs how I suggest you approach your workouts, no matter the distance or type.

You want to break the workout into two phases. The first phase comprises the first two thirds of the workout. This is what Halberg called the "transportation phase," because its purpose is simply to get you to the last third of the workout. This doesn't mean you can slack off—this part of the workout still may be challenging—but the real focus comes in the last third, which I call the "big bang phase."

This last phase of the workout is where you get the most "bang for your buck." You need to raise your intensity and really focus here, the same way you would toward the end of a race. You're going to be tired—that's the point!

The challenge in the big bang phase can come in a number of different forms. There's the challenge of duration, where it's all you can do to keep going. You might be challenged to maintain a difficult pace, or perhaps even increase it. Your challenge might be to maintain good form despite how tired you feel. No matter the physical challenge, however, you will face the same mental challenge: You must not hold a pity party. You're training faster to race faster. Lean into it and embrace the suffering.

One point to clarify: The big bang phase is not necessarily the part of the workout where you run faster. It might be about running faster, but it's ultimately about executing the purpose of the workout (duration, pace, or form) without giving up.

Finally, be wary of running too fast in the transportation phase of the workout. The purpose of the transportation phase is to produce the appropriate level of physical and mental fatigue based on the goal of the workout. You're aiming for just the right balance: You want to be fresh, but not too fresh; tired, but not too tired. If you're feeling good that day, then this might mean holding back a little during the first two thirds of the workout. That's okay! Your focus should be on the big bang phase, so just get there and then tackle it head-on.

Lesson #14: Keep Easy Runs Easy

If it's been said once, it's been said a thousand times: In order to get the best out of yourself in training (in those big bang workout sessions!), it's essential to *keep your easy runs easy* so you can run your hard runs hard. However, a lot of runners have trouble doing this. They feel good, or they're afraid running easy won't keep them fit . . . or they might not know *how* to run easy.

Those first two hurdles simply require discipline and confidence, but this last obstacle—not knowing what "running easy" really means—requires some instruction.

No matter what kind of runner you are, whether you like gadgets and technology or not, you have to breathe. That's why I tell my runners that yes, while they can monitor their pace, or heart rate, or power output, the primary "metric" they should be monitoring is their breath. On your easy runs, you should be able to hold a conversation, or even a monologue, with no problem—the effort should be *that* easy. As soon as you start panting, slow it down.

The reason I recommend breath over pace is because, as we covered in *Lesson #4: Obey Your Stress/Rest Cycle*, not every day is the same. You could be running the same pace as yesterday, but because of life stress, or weather, or any number of factors, it could feel a lot harder—and on easy days, the point is to let your body recover, not to put more undue stress on it. So paying attention to how you feel over numbers on a watch will help you keep yourself in check.

Some runners, especially those coming from triathlon, like to use heart rate to judge their effort. This can be a useful, objective metric, but the issue is that it's not your heart—or even your cardiovascular system in general—that is the limiting factor on your fitness, it's your musculoskeletal system. (Remember *Lesson #2: The Most Important Training Lesson*?) Put another way, what tends to get injured, your lungs or your legs? If you were to train solely by heart rate, the fitter you got, the faster you could run while maintaining a low heart rate. But is your musculoskeletal system ready to withstand the impact of all that faster running? It's hard to know, because while we have a heart rate monitor, we don't have a musculoskeletal monitor! Therefore, the simplest metric I've found that runners can use is their breath (just like we talked about in *Lesson #6: Talk Test*).

Lesson #15: Recovery Days

Now we come to many runners' least-favorite topic: rest and recovery.

If you are anything like me, taking days off from running can be a challenge. We not only live in a culture where "more is better," but we, as runners, are competitive. We want to be the best! If we're not running, it feels like we're being lazy. Surely our competitors aren't being lazy!

However, the reality is that if you're properly obeying your stress/rest cycle, then more is not always better. In fact, too much running can oftentimes prevent you from reaching your running goals. It may sound counterintuitive, but I'm going to argue that taking recovery days—or even days where you don't run at all—will actually help you become the best runner you can be.

The most important thing to understand is that recovery days give your body a break from the pounding of hard running—something it needs to avoid injury. Taking a recovery day also allows your body to absorb the training you have been doing. You may actually see a fitness boost following a day of recovery! So rather than viewing these easy running or nonrunning days as "punishment" or "slacking," think about them as an important part of your training.

. . . and that means putting them on the schedule! All of the plans I make for my athletes include recovery days, because I know runners are more likely to adhere to them if they're in black and white on the schedule.

In keeping with *Lessons #4: Obey Your Stress/Rest Cycle*, I give my athletes three different choices for their recovery days: easy running, cross-training, or complete rest. There are several reasons why I provide these options rather than dictating what I think they should do. First, every runner's frequency—that is, how many days they like to run each week—is specific to them. For example, maybe you find that your sweet spot is running five days per week. In a plan that has four days of scheduled running and three recovery days, you then have the flexibility to run on one of those recovery days and cross-train or rest the other two.

Second, having options means you have the freedom to listen to what your body needs on that day. If you are feeling fresh and good, maybe you'll run five to six days a week, instead of four to five. However, if you have an ache or a pain that seems like it could turn into an injury, you can scale back on the running while still following your training plan by using your recovery days to cross-train or rest instead of run.

Third, runners often have other athletic interests too! If you really like rock climbing, or swimming, or tennis, then having flexible recovery days gives you the opportunity to work those other sports into your schedule without sacrificing your running plan.

Finally, having flexibility with your recovery days makes it easier to stay consistent despite a hectic or disrupted life schedule. For instance, maybe you have a trip coming up where you need to leave very early, and you know you'll be arriving to your destination late. If you schedule a recovery day for that day of travel, then you won't be stressed about trying to squeeze a run in while it's dark; instead, you can feel confident in your choice to cross-train in the hotel gym or take the day off, all without feeling guilty for not running. All you have to do is look ahead and plan accordingly.

One last piece of rest-day advice for those rehabbing an injury: When you feel ready to return to running, give yourself one extra day of rest. One more day won't matter in the grand scheme of things, and it will really help to fortify your body before you start training again. This same principle applies with any nagging ache or pain—if you have to question the run, just take a rest day and try again tomorrow. You will never regret one day off if it means that you can keep running healthy and injury free.

Lesson #16: Adjusting Workouts for "Off" Days

Every runner goes into a workout hoping for the best. We all want to feel great and hit our planned paces. The reality, however, is that you're likely to have a few workouts where you just don't feel good. Or you may show up to the track for your workout and find that the wind is howling. Or maybe the heat index is so high that your body can't cope. What's a runner to do?

One difference between pro runners and amateurs is that pro runners (often with the wisdom of their coaches) learn to be comfortable with adjusting their expectations for compromised workouts. This openness to reconfiguring a workout when things aren't optimal allows pro runners to make the otherwise compromised workout a positive training session. Where many recreational runners will throw in the towel and begin a slippery slope of frustration because they "failed" the workout, pro runners have the ability to turn a "lemon" workout into lemonade.

Let's use this example: You have a workout of six 800-meter repeats at 10K pace with a 2-minute recovery jog. You don't feel great at the start, but you decide to give it a try. (Note that, as we discussed in the Q&A following *Lesson #12: Which Runner Showed Up Today?*, this is a good idea, because a lot of times runners don't feel great at the start of a workout, but then by mid-workout they've loosened up and the feeling has passed.) A few reps in, you've confirmed that you're having an "off" day. The best option in this situation is, if possible, to delay the workout to another day, one when you hopefully feel better. Let's say, however, that you can't move the workout. If you're following the example of pro runners, you'll adjust the workout in one of three ways.

First, and the best option for 10K runners up to marathoners, is to slow the goal time for each repeat. If your ideal training pace for this workout is 8:30/mile, shoot instead for around 8:40/mile (a 2.5% adjustment using the chart below). Then you can settle in and complete the workout feeling good that you salvaged what could have been a disastrous day. In this case, it's all about effort level; pro runners know that pushing to hit the original pace on this kind of day will result in overtraining.

Better to adjust the workout and get the work in at the effort level that was intended for the day. The pros are confident that when they put in the right effort, they will see positive adaptations, and you should be confident of this too.

A second option is to adjust the number of repeats. So instead of doing six repeats, which would require too much effort in tough circumstances, you would run three to four repeats at the goal pace and call it a day. This is the best option if you're concentrating on shorter distances, from 800m to 5K, because practicing running fast is of critical importance. Running the prescribed pace allows you to get in some work at a fast pace, but modifying the volume of fast running keeps you from overdoing it and then needing extended recovery after the workout.

The third and final option can be paired with either of the first two options or executed on its own: Increase the recovery time between repeats. In our example, instead of taking 2 minutes between each repeat, you could take 3 or 4 minutes. This is a good option if you are trying to keep your mileage up (so you want to get in all the reps) but it's equally important to hit your paces (say, in a workout leading up to a race). Just keep in mind that this is not true of all workouts; some workouts are meant to fatigue you and test your mental stamina. In those cases, it's much more about effort and less about exact pace, so you wouldn't want to extend your recovery time in that case.

Again, pro runners are comfortable making these adjustments to ensure a positive workout, and they are confident about making these adjustments on the fly—meaning not just before they begin the workout, but mid-workout as well—based on how they feel and how they are performing. We amateurs should get more comfortable making these "compromises" too.

Quick Recap: Four Levels of Workout Adjustment

	Body Sensations	Headwind	Heat Index	Adjustment
Level 1	A little off, not too bad	Slight	80+	2.5% reduction
Level 2	Heavy legs, lacking "snap"	Moderate	90+	4% reduction

| Level 3 | Slow and tired; legs are dead | Strong | 100+ | 6% reduction |
| Level 4 | Sick or on the verge of injury; no physical/ mental energy | So strong you have to lean forward to move | 105+ | Bag the workout. Take the day off or jog easy |

Coach Q&A: How do I know whether or not to adjust (or skip) a workout?

Runners hate to hear this, but if you're questioning whether to adjust or skip a workout, one of the best guides is your gut. Call this your intuition, your emotion, your "internal coach"—call it whatever you want, but it's usually pretty good at knowing what to do. Of course, all the while your brain is shouting "You're lazy!" and "It's on the schedule, slacker," but to make the right call, you need to go deeper than that. Your gut will tell you: If you're just being lazy, you'll know, which means you need to get out there and do the work. On the other hand, if something is really wrong or pushing forward might put you in jeopardy, your gut will tell you that too. *Listen.*

PREHAB TRAINING

No More Injuries!

"Prehab" is a term I learned from the great running therapist Phil Wharton. The idea is that you do *pre*habilitation to keep your body working so you don't have to do *re*habilitation because you are injured.

Once I implemented the lessons I learned from Phil (and from many of the top therapists in the world while I worked at the Olympic level), the injury rate in my runners went down. And not just a little bit, a lot.

The injury rate for my runners plummeted by over 80%. That's right: With just a few simple methods, you can reduce your injury rate by over 80%. This is very important, because most surveys show that 50–70% of all runners get injured each year. Injuries stall your fitness development and take you away from the sport you love. In this section, I'll show you how to virtually erase running injuries from your life.

Lesson #17: What Prehab Type Are You?

The first key aspect of prehab training is understanding yourself.

As a coach, one of the first things I do with runners is try to figure out their "prehab type" (kind of like identifying runner type—Speedster, Combo Runner, or Endurance Monster—before settling on a training plan). I categorize athletes into three basic "prehab personality" types:

The Minimalist simply wants to run. Okay, most of us just want to run, but this runner actively avoids anything extra that doesn't have to do with running. He simply will not invest the time.

The goal for Minimalists is to find one or two exercises that require very little equipment or time and target the runner's most often-injured areas. This will give him the most "bang for his buck," and keeping the number of exercises down will help to ensure that he can form the habit and stick with it. I definitely fall into this category.

The Sometimes-er knows she *should* do strength and mobility exercises—in fact, she probably owns a whole bin full of recovery tools. The trouble is that she isn't super consistent. Once she gets started on a routine, she enjoys it, but she isn't always sure what would be the best use of her time, and it's easy for her to get distracted and then go several weeks without doing anything.

The key for this runner is to "use what she has." Like the minimalist, the best thing to do is to start with one to two exercises she can commit to after every run and then build from there. Because she isn't so opposed to this type of ancillary work, it will be easier for a Sometimes-er to add in core and strength routines, especially if they're part of a program someone else develops and if they apply directly to running (which is the thing she cares about!). At McMillan Running, we offer the "Marathon Legs" program for this exact type of runner—it is efficient, effective, requires minimal equipment or space, and is specifically geared toward helping runners improve their single-leg stance and movements (meaning it's specific to running).

The Gym Rat doesn't need to be convinced to work on strength; she already loves the gym and has a regular routine established. The challenge for this runner is that oftentimes the routine she loves is not geared toward running and is therefore not really helping her progress in the sport. CrossFit, for instance, will get you fit, but not necessarily runner-fit, and because the goal in CrossFit is to take the muscles to failure, it can actually fatigue you to the point where you jeopardize your next running workout.

On the plus side, this runner is usually already familiar with gym equipment and the proper form needed to push, pull, press, or lift it. For this runner, McMillan Running offers a program called "Strength in Stride," which takes the Gym Rat's knowledge and skills and applies them to running-specific exercises. (You can find "Strength in Stride," "Marathon Legs," and other programs at www.mcmillanrunning.com.)

So which "prehab personality" are you? Identifying who you are and what you prefer when it comes to strength and mobility is key, because so many runners see what others are doing online and try to fit themselves into whatever looks like the "best" mold. Maybe you've read that "all runners should do Olympic lifts," so you feel like you should do them, too. But you hate the gym, know nothing about lifting, and barely have enough time to squeeze in your post-run calf mobility. If you try to force yourself into the "must do Olympic lifts" mold, you'll most likely (a) succeed but be miserable every time you have to drag yourself to the gym, or (b) lose motivation, stop doing the lifts, and feel like a failure. Neither option sounds very fun.

Instead, look at what you like and don't like to do, how much time you have available, and what your body needs. (And remember: Not all bodies are the same! So what works for your friend or your running idol won't necessarily work for you.) Then, fashion your strength and mobility work around those elements. It sounds cheesy, but finding the prehab routine that works best for *you* is what will set you up for success.

Lesson #18: Simplifying Prehab

Even once you know your prehab type, it can be overwhelming to try and pick a routine. There are dozens and dozens of routines on YouTube, articles in magazines, and anecdotal advice galore. How can you possibly determine what will keep *you* from getting injured?

Step one is to use the training lessons we just covered in the first two sections of this book. As was mentioned over and over, you must adjust your training as you go based on how your body is feeling. Do this effectively, and no tightness, ache, or pain should become an injury. (And we all know that cycle: A body part gets tight. Then, it or an adjacent body part starts to hurt. Then we ignore the pain for several days, resulting in the whole area getting injured and forcing us to take time off.) The goal in this section of the book is to stop the injury cycle in its tracks. Modifying your training is a big key to doing that.

Step two is to try out three basic prehab routines, which I'm going to share with you next.

Every runner is different—different bodies, different needs, different preferences—but across the thousands of athletes I've trained, these three routines will give you the best results with the least time investment. Be open to trying other prehab routines—especially if a healthcare professional assigns you something to prevent a specific recurring injury—but make sure you still cover the principles of the following three.

Lesson #19: Mobility Prehab Routine

First we called it "stretching." Then, the word "stretching" went out of fashion and we started calling it "flexibility." Soon, "flexibility" was no longer in vogue, and we started calling it "mobility." And I have to admit, I do like "mobility" best, as it gets at the end goal (optimal mobility) as opposed to the process used (stretching).

No matter what you call it, the point is that your tissues must operate properly to move your joints through the desired range of motion without dysfunction. Every therapist in the world will tell you that your injuries are the result of some kind of dysfunction as you try to move your body across the earth on two legs.

The challenge is that the simple act of putting one foot in front of the other requires a complex coordination of several body systems, and a hiccup in one system can create a domino effect that results in aches and pains close to or sometimes far away from where the hiccup actually occurs.

For example, I was recently working with Tom on his form. He was plagued by calf injuries, so we were trying to tease out where the problem might be coming from. He warmed up, and I fired up the video camera.

As he ran his easy pace, everything looked good. But as he moved to marathon race pace and then to half-marathon race pace, we saw something interesting. As the pace got faster, his hip rotation increased. We could see it on the video and later confirmed it in the lab. When he picked up the pace, he was no longer able to hold his hips stable while his legs moved underneath.

Tom knew he had tight hips, but here was the proof: As he tried to run his race pace, his lack of hip mobility forced his body to "cheat" and his hips to rotate to try and get the extra range of motion needed for the pace.

And guess what can happen when your hips must start twisting to get more range of motion? That's right: a domino effect. This twisting can cause extra torque and dysfunction throughout the body, particularly down where the body interacts with the ground. For Tom, it manifested in his calves. They became overworked, and his physical therapist confirmed that while the calves themselves were grumpy, it was his tight hip flexors leading to the extra hip rotation that was probably the root cause of all of his calf problems.

Our next step? Helping Tom gain more hip mobility so that at training and race paces, his hip rotation would stay in an optimal zone.

Mobility Influencers

Mobility is influenced by: (1) your fascia; (2) your nervous system; (3) your soft tissues (muscles, tendons and ligaments); and (4) your joint structure (how the bones interact). (And, at times, scar tissue.) In my opinion, this is the reason "stretching" has always been a hotly debated topic. Depending on which of these four influencers is most affecting your particular problem, your "stretching" program might not be the right one to solve the issue.

For example, let's say that your hamstring feels tight. To loosen it, you try stretching to lengthen the muscle itself. However, the muscle may not be the problem; it could be that your nervous system is actually holding the muscle tight. In other words, you may in fact have optimal flexibility in your hamstring, but you can't get the nervous system to relax in order to let the muscle relax. As a result, you stretch and stretch and stretch and get very little relief. (You might even find that the muscle seems to get *tighter*.) Sound familiar?

In this case, if you had done mobility work that addressed the nervous system as well as the tissue itself (active isolated flexibility, in this case), you would likely have gotten relief. In this way, you would have properly matched the mobility routine with the issue causing the dysfunction.

Getting Started with Mobility

Over time, you'll learn the exact mobility movements that help you avoid injury and perform your best. To get you started, I'm going to share my favorite active isolated mobility exercises.

Active isolated mobility utilizes something called "reciprocal inhibition" to turn off the nervous system input that holds a muscle tight and allow the muscle to relax. Basically, you contract one muscle group so the opposing muscle relaxes. Using your hands or a rope or strap, you provide a slight assist at the point where you start to feel a stretch, hold for 1–2 seconds, then return to the starting position. (I get athletes to count bananas, so they don't go too fast. *One banana... Two bananas...*) Really pay attention to your body when you are doing these exercises, and never pull or push farther than your limb will go. We don't want to overstretch the muscles; we want them to naturally relax and lengthen, which takes time, repetition, and patience.

Perform each of the following exercises for 20–25 repetitions on one leg, and then switch legs. If done three to five times per week *after* your runs, over two to three months you'll experience a more fluid stride, and many common aches and pains will go away.

Active Isolated Mobility Routine: Six Key Exercises

How to: Lay on your back with your legs flat on the floor. Draw one knee toward your chest and grasp your knee to assist the final part of the movement. Hold for 1-2 seconds. Return to the starting position.

Form notes: Play around with the direction of the knee to find tight areas. Do some repetitions with the knee moving toward your armpit and some with the knee moving toward the center of your chest. Experiment to find the movements where you feel restriction and do your final repetitions there.

Hamstring – Bent Leg

How to: Lay on your back and bend your knees so your feet are flat on the floor. With the knee staying bent, raise one leg until the thigh is perpendicular to the ground. Hold the leg at the knee and slowly extend the leg toward the ceiling. Once you feel a slight stretch, hold for 1–2 seconds and return to the starting position.

Form notes: Don't worry if you can't get your leg fully straight. Just find the point of slight resistance and, over time, you'll be able to get the leg straighter as optimal mobility returns.

Hamstring – Straight Leg

How to: Lay on your back with one leg flat on the floor and the other bent at the knee so that foot is flat. Wrap the strap around the arch of the straight-legged foot. Raise that leg toward the ceiling and use the strap to assist in the final part of the movement. Once you feel a slight stretch, hold for 1-2 seconds and return to the starting position.

Form notes: As with the last exercise, don't worry if you can't get your leg to perpendicular to the floor. And do not pull with the strap! It's only meant to give a slight assist. Be patient— your range of motion will improve over time as long as you don't overstretch the muscle.

Hip Flexor

How to: Standing with one hand on a chair or against a wall for balance, bend one knee so your foot comes up behind you, and grasp just above your ankle. As you contract your glute, gently pull the foot to assist the movement of the foot toward the glute. Hold for 1–2 seconds and return to the starting position.

Form notes: Be careful not to arch your back to get more movement. Use the glute/hamstring to work within your available range of motion.

Calves – Straight Leg

How to: Sit with your legs extended. Wrap a strap around the arch of one foot. Contract your shin muscle to pull the top of your foot toward you. Use the strap to assist in the final part of the movement. Once a slight stretch is felt, hold for 1–2 seconds and return to the starting position.

Form notes: Play around with the direction of the foot to find tight areas. Do some repetitions with the foot moving straight toward you, some with the foot turned in (inverted) and some with the foot turned out (everted). Experiment to find the movements where you feel restriction, and do your final repetitions there.

Calves – Bent Leg

How to: Sit with your knees bent and feet flat on the floor. Contract one shin muscle to pull the top of that foot toward you. Use your hands to assist in the final part of the movement. Once a slight stretch is felt, hold for 1–2 seconds and return to the starting position.

Form notes: As with the straight-leg exercise, play around with the direction of the foot to find tight areas. Do your final repetitions in the directions where you find the most restriction.

Final Thoughts

This routine should work well to get you started on your journey to creating an optimal mobility routine. Like most things in running, it takes some trial and error to see what works best for you, and that routine may be different than what works best for your training partners. The bottom line is that mobility seems to be a key to overall health and to helping your body move in an appropriate way. Moreover, I firmly believe that mobility work is the best diagnostic tool runners can use to find issues before they become an ache/pain or injury.

I'm going to say that again: In my mind, the point of mobility work is not necessarily to give you extra flexibility, but to do a daily diagnostic check of your body to find and address tight areas before they start to ache or cause pain.

In other words, do your mobility!

Finally, as you experiment to find what works for you, I highly suggest checking out Coach Angela's 3HAB and Magic Mobility programs. These follow-along videos are available on www.mcmillanrunning.com.

Quick Recap: 6 Key Mobility Exercises

Here is a summary of the six key mobility exercises. Remember to hold each exercise for 1–2 seconds at the farthest point your body will allow (without overstretching!) before returning to the starting position. Repeat 20–25 times on each leg.

Key Movement	How to
Low Back / Glute Release	Lay on your back with legs flat on floor. Draw one knee toward your chest and grasp knee to assist the final part of the movement. Hold for 1-2 seconds. Return to starting position.
Hamstring – Bent Leg	Lay on your back with legs flat on floor. With bent knee, raise one leg until thigh is perpendicular to the ground. Hold the leg at the knee and slowly extend leg toward the ceiling. Once a slight stretch is felt, hold for 1-2 seconds and return to starting

	position.
Hamstring – Straight Leg	Lay on your back with one leg flat on floor and the other bent so the foot is flat. Raise the straight leg toward the ceiling and use a strap to assist in the final part of the movement. Once a slight stretch is felt, hold for 1-2 seconds and return to starting position.
Hip Flexor	Standing on two feet, bend one knee to grasp the leg near the ankle. Contract the glute and hamstring of the bent leg and move it backwards so foot moves toward glute. Once a slight stretch is felt, hold for 1-2 seconds and return to starting position.
Calves – Straight Leg	Sit with legs extended. Wrap a strap around the arch of one foot. Contract that shin muscle to pull the foot toward you. Use the strap to assist in the final part of the movement. Once a slight stretch is felt, hold for 1-2 seconds and return to starting position.
Calves – Bent Leg	Sit with knees bent and feet flat on floor. Contract one shin muscle to pull the foot toward you. Use your hands to assist in the final part of the movement. Once a slight stretch is felt, hold for 1-2 seconds and return to starting position.

The answer—which will sound familiar by now—is, "It depends." It depends on what your issue is and what you prefer.

For oft-injured runners, runners who feel "tight," or those who just want to be more prepared for their run, it is recommended that you do some myofascial movements (like foam rolling) and active isolated or similar dynamic mobility movements before each run. A movement-oriented routine prepares the tissues for your upcoming run and may help your tight areas loosen. Static stretching (where you hold the muscle in a lengthened position for 30–60 seconds) is not advisable before a run unless directed by your physical therapist.

For all runners, it is recommended that you perform myofascial, active isolated, and/or integrated movements like traditional mobility or yoga after each of your runs. At this point, your tissues are fully warmed up and most receptive to mobility work.

Again, to find exact routines and videos to follow, head to www.mcmillanrunning.com and look for the Magic Mobility, 3HAB, and Yoga Recovery Routines. Or join the McMillan Run Team and I'll incorporate the routines right into your training plan.

Lesson #20: Core Prehab Routine

I created the Runner's Core Routine back before core training was as ubiquitous for runners as it is today. I experimented with my runners over the years and whittled down all of the various core exercises to the ones that I found were the most effective. Most runners are time-starved when it comes to prehab training, so it was essential not only that the core routine did its job but that it didn't require a ton of time or equipment.

By now, thousands and thousands of runners have used the Runner's Core Routine, and I'm happy to present it to you here. Note: Video is really the best way to learn the routine, so while I'm going to describe the key exercises in Stage 1 here, you can watch more thorough videos and progress to more advanced Stages 2 and 3 by visiting www.mcmillanrunning.com and signing up for the Runner's Core Routine.

Stage 1 of the Runner's Core Routine is essentially my core stability field test: The exercises are arranged to illuminate your strengths and weaknesses. You'll likely find some of the exercises pretty easy to complete, while the difficulty of others will surprise you. This is the point of Stage 1; I want you to find those weaker areas, so you know where you need to put extra attention. Again, we're trying to be hyper-efficient so you are more likely to get the routine done.

Here are the seven key exercises that make up Stage 1 of the Runner's Core Routine.

Core Routine: Seven Key Exercises

Front Plank

How to: Start in a push-up position, resting on your elbows. Raise your hips off the ground and hold your body straight— literally like a plank of wood. Hold for 10 seconds, then lower your hips and rest for 10 seconds. Repeat three times so you hold the plank position for 30 seconds total.

Form notes: Make sure your body is in a straight line from ears to ankles. Common errors include dropping your head or arching or swaying your back. Avoid these errors by using a floor mirror or having a partner watch and point out when you lose form.

Side Plank

How to: Still on the floor, prop your body up on one elbow and place your feet heel-to-toe. Lift your body up so it forms a plank again, but this time sideways and perpendicular to the ground rather than parallel. Hold for 10 seconds, then lower your hips and rest for 10 seconds. Repeat three times so you hold the plank position for 30 seconds total.

Form notes: Mistakes here include tilting the body forward or rotating the hips forward or backward. If you find your form deteriorating, don't progress until you can hold that position properly.

Leg Lowering

How to: Lying on your back now, place your hands slightly under your hips and raise your legs to 90 degrees. Pull your bellybutton toward the ground, tighten your lower back against the ground, and lower both legs toward the ground. As soon as your back begins to arch, raise your legs to the starting position. This is one rep. Repeat 10 times.

Form notes: It's crucial here to keep your lower back pressed against the ground. Over time you'll be able to lower your legs even closer to the ground with each rep, but don't rush it or you will lose the benefit of the exercise.

Metronome

How to: Start in the same position as with the leg lowering exercise, but spread your arms out into a "t" shape, palms down. Lower your legs to one side, in the direction of one hand, and touch the ground with your feet. Reverse direction to repeat touching the ground on the other side. Completing both sides counts as one rep. Repeat 5 times.

Form notes: Be patient. This is often one of the hardest core exercises for runners who are new to core work.

Sit-up with a Twist

How to: On your back, knees bent, feet flat on the floor, anchor your feet under a couch or sturdy chair, or have a partner hold them down. Sit up and rotate your core so that you twist to face one side. Lower back down, and then sit up and twist to your other side. This counts as one rep. Repeat 5 times.

Form notes: Perform this exercise, especially the raising and lowering of your torso, slowly. Remember: quality over quantity!

"Jane Fonda"

How to: Lay on your side and flex your top foot so your toes come toward your face (opposite of ballerina feet). Slightly rotate that top leg inward (toward the other leg) and raise it one to two feet in the air. Return to starting position. This is one rep on one side. Repeat 10 times on each side.

Form notes: Be careful not to roll your hips or top thigh backward. The body often wants to cheat this exercise and use non-hip muscles—don't let it!

Fit Ball Balance

How to: Get a large fit ball (also called an exercise ball or Swiss ball). Using a doorway or wall for stability, climb onto the ball so you are kneeling on top. Release your grip on the doorframe/wall and balance on your knees for 5 seconds. If you don't have a fit ball, balancing (standing) on one leg and spelling "I R-U-N F-A-S-T" with the leg in the air will do the trick.

Form notes: Be careful not to fall! If you start to lose balance, use the doorframe/wall to stabilize.

Trust me, after going through the full Runner's Core Routine, you'll have all the core stability you need to run as fast as you can dream. The program is simple, effective, and efficient. Sure, there are lots of cool and extreme core exercises available (and you can do them if you like), but I find the Runner's Core Routine to be the best and safest way to build a strong, effective core.

Quick Recap: 7 Key Core Exercises

Here's a summary of the seven key exercises, along with starting reps and "build to" reps. Once you've maxed out the recommended reps on these exercises—with excellent form, of course—you can progress to Stage 2 and then Stage 3. Typically I've found that runners will spend 4–6 weeks working through each stage; any faster than that and they're likely sacrificing good form somewhere along the way.

Key Exercise	Starting Reps	"Build to" Reps	Watch out for
Front Plank	3 x 10s on/off	3 x 30s on/off	Dropping the head, arching the back
Side Plank	3 x 10s on/off (each side)	3 x 30s on/off (each side), stacking feet	Tilting or rotating hips forward or backward
Leg Lowering	10	20, lowering feet further	Arching the back
Metronome	5 (each side)	15 (each side)	Frustration (this one is hard!)
Sit-up with a Twist	5 (each side)	25 (each side)	Rushing
"Jane Fonda"	10 (each side)	25 (each side)	Rolling hips or top thigh backward
Fit Ball Balance	5s	15s	Falling

Coach Q&A: How often do I need to do core exercises?

For most runners, performing core exercises twice per week (consistently over a few months) is sufficient. But, since the core is designed to tolerate consistent work, you can pretty much perform core training as often as you like. That being said, more is not always better—especially if you end up fatigued and not able to run as well in your upcoming workouts—so pay attention to how the core workouts affect your runs so you don't overdo it.

Lesson #21: Strength Prehab Routine

The final prehab routine that I feel every runner must do is runner-specific strength training.

Admittedly, not all runners embrace strength work. "It's boring" or "It'll make me bulk up" or "I'm a runner, not a bodybuilder" are common protests I've heard over the years. In fact, the exercises themselves won't necessarily make you faster, which might make you wonder: "What's the point?"

The point of strength work is to prevent or correct imbalances runners develop from hours and hours of running, and to build up resiliency in our bodies so we can endure all of that pounding. The more resilient and balanced you are, the less you'll get injured, which means more consistent, high-level running training, which *will* make you faster. As I like to say: This is the training that allows you to do the training.

Strength Routine: Five Key Exercises

As with mobility and core training, there are dozens and dozens of strength programs available and just as many runners/coaches that feel each is the best. What I want to present are the top five movements I think every runner should master. These come from certified strength coach Angela Tieri, whom I regard as one of the world's best strength coaches for runners. The best part is that she's not just a strength coach, she's a really good runner who is also a strength coach. That means she's not the typical strength coach who adapts programs for runners; she knows how strength training feels for the runner and how it affects upcoming training. She knows that the best strength training for runners gels with your run training. The result is a set of strength routines (all found on www.mcmillanrunning.com) that are second to none for helping you become a better runner.

Single-Leg Deadlift

How to: Stand on one leg with a slight bend in the knee. Standing tall, engage your core (think about pulling your ribs down) and hinge forward so that your free leg comes straight back behind you and your torso comes forward parallel with the ground. Squeeze the glute of the standing leg to raise your torso back up to standing. Repeat 6–8 times and switch legs.

Form notes: Make sure to maintain a strong, flat back throughout this whole movement. Think about keeping your chest lifted very slightly, so you have a slight arch in your lower back (this is to avoid rounding, which is what we don't want). The other common mistake is allowing the hip of the floating leg to lift up; try to keep your hips level the whole time.

Rear-Foot Elevated Split Squat

How to: Find a stool, chair, or bench that is 6–12 inches off of the ground. Facing away from the object, rest one foot on its surface, either with your toes flat or tucked (whatever is more comfortable). Step the other foot out about two feet and drop down into a lunge so the back knee lowers to the ground (or as close as possible). Push into the ground with the heel and big toe of the standing foot, squeeze your glute, and stand up. Repeat 6–8 times and switch legs.

Form notes: Keep your front knee pointing straight forward; don't let it drift inward. Also, watch that your knee doesn't move past your toes; if it does, step that foot forward a little more. Finally, your torso should lean forward a little, but make sure you don't arch or round your back.

Chin-up

How to: This is the one exercise where you need equipment to perform. If you don't belong to a gym with a chin-up/pull-up bar, check your local playground. Monkey bars can work great!

Grip the bar with your palms facing you, hands slightly wider than your shoulders. Hang from the bar and pull yourself up, leading with your chest, until your chin touches the bar; then return to the starting position.

If you cannot get your chin to the bar at first, loop a resistance band over the bar and step into it so the band will help pull you up. Alternatively, you can start with eccentric pull-ups: Use a box or stool to step up and start at top so your chin is already at the bar. Lift your legs off of the box and lower as slowly as you can. Once you can do 6–8 eccentric or assisted chin-ups, you can progress to try full, unassisted chin-ups. Women should typically aim for three sets of 2–3 chin-ups, while men should aim for three sets of 5–6.

Form notes: As you pull up, be careful that your shoulders don't round forward and that you don't arch your back.

Step-up

How to: Find a 12–18-inch step or box. Start with one foot on the box, with both feet pointing straight ahead. Lean forward slightly, into the front leg. Then, careful not to push off of the back leg, use the glute and quad of the bent leg to lift your body into a standing position on the box. If you can maintain balance, pull the other knee up into a knee drive position; then slowly lower with control, land softly, and repeat 6–8 times before switching legs.

Form notes: A common error is letting the knee of the leg that's bent drift inward—keep that kneecap straight! Also keep your hips square so they don't drift side to side, and remember not to launch off of the back leg.

Lateral Lunge

How to: Keeping your feet parallel, toes forward, lunge out to one side and land with your foot, knee, and hip all aligned (foot under knee under hip). Keeping your chest up, sit your hips backward as you lower into the lunge. Then, pushing from the inside edge of the lunged foot, use that glute to come back up to standing. Repeat 6–8 times and switch legs.

Form notes: It's really important to make sure you're sitting back as you do this exercise, rather than leaning forward. Your torso is the limiting factor, so stop when you find your back starting to round. Also try not to step out too far—you don't want your foot to extend farther than that hip. Finally, watch your feet; they tend to try to turn out, but you want them to point forward the whole time.

To really round out your strength training, I highly recommend Coach Angela's Marathon Legs and Strength in Stride routines. You can find them on www.mcmillanrunning.com. As with all of her programs, she built them to require little to no equipment, to be safe and easy to perform (even without a strength coach watching you), and to require very little time. Big bang. Low risk. Little time commitment. Highly effective. I'd call that a quadruple-win.

Quick Recap: 5 Key Strength Exercises

Here's a summary of the five key strength exercises, along with starting reps and "build to" reps. To make things even more challenging, you can add weight, as indicated below. Anytime you add weight, drop back down to 6–8 reps and build again from there.

Key Exercise	Starting Reps	"Build to" Reps	Adding Weight	Watch out for
Single-Leg Deadlift	6–8 each leg	12 each leg	Hold one dumbbell (or other weight) in both hands; progress to holding it in one hand (same side as airborne leg)	Rounded back, unlevel hips
Rear-Foot Elevated Split Squat	6–8 each leg	12 each leg	Hold dumbbells (or other weights) in each hand; may also wear a weighted backpack on the front of body	Knee drifting inward or beyond toes, rounded/arched back
Chin-up	6–8 assisted or eccentric	3 sets of: 2–3 (women) or 5–6 (men)	n/a	Rounded shoulders, arched back
Step-up	6–8 each leg	12 each leg	See Rear-Foot Elevated Split Squat (above); Can also make the step higher to increase the challenge	Knee drifting inward, hips moving laterally, pushing off rear leg

Lateral Lunge	6–8 each leg	12 each leg	Hold dumbbells (or other weights) in each hand	Leaning too far forward, rounded back, feet turning out

Coach Q&A: How do I fit strength work in around my running?

As I seem to say in every section of the book: It depends. For many runners, doing strength work on the same day as your harder runs (either immediately after or, ideally, a few hours later) is the best timing. Coach Angela likes to stack all the stress from training on one day so the following recovery days allow you to supercompensate and perform better in upcoming hard workouts. That said, this rhythm doesn't work for all runners. Some need to do their strength training on easy days, due to either time availability or how they feel. So play around with your strength training. Over time, you'll learn which exercises and when you choose to perform them negatively affect your running. You can then develop the ideal rhythm for you, and this will keep you motivated and moving toward your goal.

Lesson #22: Interrupt the Injury Cycle

As I've mentioned, we do prehab training—namely mobility, core, and strength work—in order to continue to do the training we really want to do: running. However, just mindlessly performing these routines and continuing to run through tightness, aches, and pains will not get you the results that you want.

Most injuries develop the same way: You feel a tightness somewhere as the result of a dysfunction in the body tissues, likely in the muscle, tendon, or fascia tissues. If you don't address that tightness, it progresses to become an ache or a pain. Then if you continue to ignore that, it leads to a full-blown injury that sidelines you from running.

What we want to do is to interrupt this pathway as early as we possibly can.

The first thing to do, as I mentioned back in *Lesson #19: Mobility Prehab Routine,* is to use mobility work to find the areas of your body that are tight. Think of it as your own

174

personal MRI machine, letting you peer inside your body and find the spots that, if you ignore them, might lead to injuries. Focus on the areas that you find, and give them extra attention.

If that doesn't alleviate the tightness and you find it progressing to become an ache or pain, it's time to do the following for one to three days:

- Reduce your training load (volume of running) by 25–50%. This will give your body the time it needs to fully recover. During this time, you can substitute low-impact cross-training to encourage blood flow and keep yourself limber.
- When you do run, avoid anything that makes the ache or pain worse. For instance, if running uphill makes your calf hurt worse, stick to flat running.
- See a body worker for treatment. This can be a physical therapist, masseuse, chiropractor, acupuncturist, etc. These are people who are experts in manipulating bodies. If you can, find one who specializes in working with runners.
- Do your mobility work two to four times a day.
- Reduce inflammation by taking an ice bath one to two times per day, avoiding foods that cause inflammation,

and taking anti-inflammatory medicine (if you choose and/or are instructed by your doctor).

- Do things that make you smile and laugh as much as possible. This helps to reduce your stress hormones so that your body can recover faster.
- Prioritize sleep. Your body does a huge amount of self-repair when you sleep, so make sure you're getting at least 8–10 hours. (And any time you can lay down, lay down. Rest. Rest. Rest.)

After completing that regimen of treatment for one to three days, ease (don't rush) back into regular training. I often have runners go out on day four and walk for 5 minutes. If all feels good, they then jog slowly for 10 minutes. If everything still feels good, they walk for 5 more minutes. That's it—just a short test run to see how things are feeling. Usually they are feeling fine, so we take the next three to four days to gradually ramp back up to their normal training level.

If you find that those one to three days of treatment don't do the trick, it's time to reduce the training load even more. Take your already-reduced training volume and cut it by another 50–100% for one to three more days, and follow the same treatment protocol. After that, if things feel better, you can return to the 25–50% level of training for one to three days before easing back into full training.

Ninety-nine percent of the time, if you follow this proactive injury-interruption strategy, you will be back to training pain- and tightness-free in no time. And of course, none of us like to reduce our training, but I can promise you that it will not hurt your fitness to have a slight temporary reduction. What *will* hurt your training is letting a small issue turn into a sidelining injury that takes you out for weeks or months. Don't let it get to that point.

Lesson #23: Return from Injury: Cross-Training

We've talked plenty about preventing injury, and hopefully, if you're following all of the lessons in this chapter, you won't get injured. The reality is, though, that in sport, injuries happen.

Most injured runners' biggest fear is losing the fitness they've worked so hard to build up, so they immediately look for an alternative to running. Cross-training is a great way to stay fit and speed up recovery via improved blood flow and greater mental engagement. However, not all cross-training is equal, and it's especially important to choose a modality that works with your current stage of injury.

Phase 1: Early Stages of Injury—Avoid Pain

As any physical therapist will tell you, in the early stages of your recovery, you must choose a cross-training option where you can exercise pain-free and let the injured area heal. The logic is pretty straightforward: Why would you do something to aggravate the injured area and delay healing? In most cases, your pain-free options will *not* closely match running.

Swimming and cycling, both of which are non-weight-bearing, are often good choices.

Phase 2: Recovery Has Begun—Non-Weight-Bearing

As your injury heals and you move toward your return to running, it's time to start introducing cross-training activities that replicate the same movements as running. If you still need to avoid weight-bearing exercise during this time, aqua jogging (running in water replicating the running motion) is a great choice.

Phase 3: Recovery Is Progressing—Weight-Bearing

Once you can tolerate some weight-bearing, then the best running-specific cross-training activity is the AlterG treadmill. This is a treadmill that allows you to run, supported, at varying percentages of your body weight. For example, you can set the machine so that you are running at 80% of your body weight— thus reducing stress on the injured tissue, but still running. You would start at a level where you can run pain-free and, as you heal, gradually increase the percentage of body weight you're using so that by the time you are fully healed, you are already running at or near 100% body weight.

If you don't have access to an AlterG, then the elliptical machine (or any elliptical-like machine) is your next best option. It is weight-bearing, and your legs move in a (sort of) running motion, yet there is no pounding. Plus, you can get your heart rate pretty high on the elliptical machine, which helps maintain some intensity among all the easy exercise you're doing while healing (which is good for the body *and* the mind!).

All Stages of Injury

As demoralizing as injuries can be, they do offer a great opportunity to do cross-training that doesn't just build aerobic fitness, but also helps loosen the body, relax the mind, and strengthen weak areas. Examples include yoga, Pilates, strength training (never stressing the injured area), and core training.

A Runner Example

Megan provides a great example of how to cross-train back from injury. She was an elite runner I coached and was prone to foot problems. One season, she got a stress fracture in her foot. Here is how we progressed back to full training—after which she went on to help our team win the National Cross-Country Championships.

Phase 1: At first, Megan couldn't put any weight on the foot. All cross-training was in the pool, aqua jogging. Because there is no musculoskeletal stress, Megan could aqua jog every day, and because aqua jogging can be very boring, I had her doing fartlek-style workouts to try to get her heart rate up and make her feel like she would in a running workout. We kept the workouts simple, like 30 x 30 seconds fast with 1 minute recovery.

Phase 2: Once Megan was cleared to begin weight-bearing activities, we moved to the elliptical and bike. Both exercises were gentle on the foot, and the elliptical was great because it allowed her to practice more running-like movements, but without landing/pounding, so there was lower stress on the foot.

Phase 3: After two weeks on the elliptical and bike, we began to incorporate low body weight running on the AlterG treadmill. We started at 75% of her body weight and, over a few weeks, slowly ramped up until she was running at 95–97% body weight on the AlterG in addition to adding short runs outside.

As you can see, Megan made a gradual yet progressive return to running that allowed her body to heal but also kept her training. Even after she was healed, we kept the AlterG as part of her weekly running just as a precaution, and Megan went on to help our team win the National Championship in Cross-Country that season.

The moral of the story is: Be patient! Recovery is not always linear, and cross-training is not a perfect substitute for running; however, if done smartly and with a gradual progression, it can help you get back to the running that you love.

FORM TRAINING

Move Better

I'm going to start by stating that, categorically, there is no one best running form. Runners come in so many different shapes, sizes, and proportions that it's simply illogical that one running form, like one training plan, would work for all runners.

That said, there are a few keys to improving your form, which should help you stay injury free, perform better, and just maybe look better in those race photos.

Before we get to the specifics, it's important to know that the best running form for you comes down to these four things:

First, the best running form for you is one that keeps you injury free. I'd much prefer to have a runner with slight form issues who is healthy than a runner with perfect running form who gets hurt all the time.

Second, the best running form for you is one that is economical. All races lasting longer than 2 minutes rely mostly on aerobic ("with oxygen") energy systems. The more economical you are (i.e., the less oxygen you need to maintain a given pace), the faster you can race. I'd much prefer to have a runner with slight form issues who is very economical than a runner with perfect running form who isn't.

Third, the best running form for you is one that gives you better top speed. A lot of the current thrust in running form changes is about the biomechanics alone. To me, however, biomechanics are third on the priority list. Yes, you want to have great biomechanics, but if you become overly injury-prone by running the "perfect" way and/or are so inefficient that you fatigue early in races, it doesn't matter that your mechanics appear to be ideal.

Lastly, my general philosophy on running form is "If it ain't broke, don't fix it!" If you are injury free, then don't do a wholesale form change. Just clean up your form using the lessons that follow.

If, however, you've done smart training and all the prehab work to build an injury-free body and yet you still get hurt, then it's time to look at making more substantial changes. Just make sure you work with a coach who understands not just running biomechanics but that your best form, above all, must keep you injury free.

Okay. Let's get to the nitty gritty.

Lesson #24: Posture

Remember when your mother used to harp on you to sit up straight? Well, if I were working with you on form, you'd hear me telling you to "run tall." This cue, *run tall*, helps get you in an upright, non-slouching posture, which is best for running. As McMillan Coach and Olympian Andrew "Lemon" Lemoncello shows in the photo below, you want your head above your shoulders, shoulders above your hips, and hips above your knees and ankles.

Modern life makes it easy for us to slouch, so fight that in running and run tall. Your mom would be proud.

Lesson #25: Arm Swing

When running, your arms should be bent at roughly 90 degrees. Your hands should be lightly clasped, and when your arms swing, your hands should brush between your lowest rib and your waistband. The swinging action itself is front-to-back and relaxed.

Any abnormal swinging (crossing the body, elbows out, shoulders high) will have consequences in your mechanics. Race photos often illuminate any arm swing issues, and you can have someone video you while running from the front and back to evaluate your arm action.

As the following photo of Lemon depicts, imagine there is a box or picture frame from your shoulders to your hips. Your arm swing should stay within this box, and your hands should not cross the midline of the body. Don't be rigid, just make sure your arms stay within the box.

Quick fixes:

- If your elbows are swinging out, stick your thumbs out

to your sides "Fonzie style." (Fonzie was a character in an old sitcom who would say "Aaah" and flip his thumbs out like a hitchhiker.) When you do this, it naturally pulls your elbows in by your sides.

– If you cross the midline with your hands/arms, carry sticks or paintbrushes in training that you can use as visual cues. (You'll see the sticks without needing to tilt your head down, or the sticks will touch, reminding you to keep them from crossing the midline of your body.)

Lesson #26: Foot Plant

There is a lot of chatter out there on foot plant. In my opinion, it matters less whether you land toward the front or the rear of your foot; what matters most is that your feet land under your body (or at least close).

Overstriding, or stepping "in front of" your body, is the main issue you want to avoid. Runners can overstride with a forefoot plant as well as a heel plant. The key is to focus on landing under you and pushing behind you. (In the photo, note that Lemon isn't reaching out but is landing under his body.)

I find that if runners think about pushing harder down into the ground and "scraping" their foot back, they cure their overstriding. Again, have someone video you (this time from the side) while you are running, and you'll see if you are landing in front of your body (overstriding) or nearly under your body (correct landing).

Lesson #27: Rhythm & Cadence

Running is a lot like dancing, in that the runners who look the best, regardless of speed, are the ones that have great rhythm and quick cadence when they run. There is a certain flow to their stride. They are relaxed and smooth. I like to say, "Run tall. Run relaxed." This simple cue usually cures most form issues and results in a great running rhythm.

Think about how amazing Olympic gold medalist Eliud Kipchoge looks when he runs. There is a relaxed rhythm to his stride. Or how about Boston Marathon Champion Des Linden? Whereas Eliud Kipchoge has long limbs and a bouncy stride, Des is more compact and yet still floats along the road with a smooth stride and effortless-looking movements. That's what we're looking to achieve with our running form.

As for cadence, researchers have suggested that a cadence (or stride frequency) of 180 steps per minute is optimal. Several argue that a lower cadence leads to injury, but the evidence isn't entirely conclusive, and the magical "180" number is based on professional athletes—which most of us aren't. That's why I would suggest that anything from 170–190 works, depending on the runner.

You can count your steps in one minute to get your cadence, or most GPS monitors now do this for you as well. If you find you need to increase your cadence, just make sure you aren't sacrificing stride length by shortening your stride too much. Understriding to achieve an optimal cadence will slow you down, whereas the whole point of a quicker cadence is to speed you up! We want an optimal stride *rate* (cadence) *and* an optimal stride *length*. They work together to create speed.

Along with posture, foot plant, and arm swing, these are just four basic tips to keep in mind if you want to work on your running form. Again, few runners need a complete overhaul of their stride; so long as you're not getting injured, you probably don't need to change much. The best form, ultimately, is the one that keeps you injury free. (Who cares if it looks ugly? Haile Gebrselassie, Olympic champion and holder of 27 world records, ran with one arm more static than the other because that's the arm he carried his books in when running to school. His form didn't look perfect, but it certainly worked for him!)

195

Once you find the form that staves off injuries, then you can work on making tweaks to improve economy (i.e., running efficiency, or the ability to preserve your energy in a race) and, finally, speed.

The previous lessons included tips on improving certain aspects of your form, but if you really want to make big gains, do running form drills and strides. We talked about strides back in *Lesson 7: Zones & Workouts*; typically you'll do these after you do the drills, so that you can incorporate the movements from the drills into some short, fast bursts of running.

As for what drills to do, I created my Drills for Distance Runners video routine as an easy way for runners, who often lack the coordination necessary for more advanced form drills, to get started. After doing the drills in this video for a few weeks, you'll see a big improvement in running form.

Head to www.mcmillanrunning.com to access the Drills for Distance Runners video routine.

Lesson #28: Video/Self-Analysis & Form Data

Knowing the fundamentals of good running form is one thing, but it can be challenging to implement them, especially if you don't know what your body is doing in space. Therefore, it's often helpful to get some feedback so you know what to work on. Today, this is very easy.

To get visual feedback, just hand your smartphone to a friend and get her to take 10-second videos of you running. Have her film you running toward and away from the camera, and have her take another video of you from the side.

See how you look. How's your posture? What about your arm swing? Most runners are amazed when they see themselves run. A quick video can provide a big inspiration to work on your mechanics.

Melissa used this technique to quickly correct her "flying elbows." When she ran, her elbows stuck out, creating a more side-to-side instead of front-to-back running motion with her arms. After seeing herself run, she was more motivated to use

199

the "Fonzie" method (similar to hitchhiker thumbs, as described in *Lesson #25: Arm Swing*) to correct her arm swing. I had Melissa do a minute or two of "Fonzie" running in each mile of her runs, and soon enough, the flying elbows were gone, and her next set of videos showed a more appropriate front-to-back arm motion.

In addition to video, you can get biomechanical feedback from many watches now too. You can easily learn your cadence, see differences between your left foot and right foot, determine your ground contact time, and more.

Finally, to get even more insights on correcting form issues that are causing injuries, visit a local biomechanics lab (typically located at universities). There the technicians can dive even deeper into your form and provide exact exercises to help you develop your most efficient, effective running form.

Whether you watch a video of yourself running, consult data from your watch, seek a full analysis at a lab, or some combination of the three, you should spend at least two to three weeks on corrective exercises and drills before you look for change in your form. (The Drills for Distance Runners video routine posted at www.mcmillanrunning.com is a good place to start.)

After performing the drills several days a week for a few weeks, take some new videos or analyze your watch data. What has improved? What else can you work on?

NUTRITION TRAINING

Feed the Machine

Nutrition is probably one of the most hotly contested aspects of running training. Everyone has an opinion, and we all want the magic bullet that is going to make us leaner/faster/stronger.

Of course, this has led to a lot of confusion. From diet trends to the latest supplement on the block, I've seen runners try it all in search of "the one thing" that will make them the fastest version of themselves. However, I'll let you in on a secret. I've worked with runners from all around the globe, runners of varying ages, runners who are racing on the track, and runners who are traversing hundreds of miles in the mountains—in short, runners of all types with different dietary preferences and access to different foods. And what I've found is that at the end of the day, feeding yourself to become a better runner is pretty darned simple. The key is to focus on the "cake."

In this analogy, the "cake" of a diet is the foundation—a healthy, balanced diet. The "icing" is the final 1% stuff: special diet tweaks, supplements, and so forth. Runners wanting to optimize their performance often focus overwhelmingly on the icing, when they should be focusing on what goes into their cake. So that's why most of what I'm about to share is all about building a really good "cake." We'll look at some nutrition basics that every runner—really, every human—should follow. Then we'll get into some runner-specific fundamentals. Finally, once you have a good strong foundation, you can head over to www.mcmillanrunning.com to read up on some of the "icing" content, like "No-Fuel/Slow-Fuel Long Runs." But remember: Get your "cake" right first!

Lesson #29: Focus on Diet Quality

If you live in Western society, you'll recognize that in this day and age, we are surrounded by more calories than our ancestors could have ever imagined. Of course, these calories are in large part delivered through processed, packaged, taste-bud-exploitive foods, so for most of us, when it comes to improving our running through diet, all we really need to do is clean it up.

A few years ago, my friend and renowned author Matt Fitzgerald released his Diet Quality Score (DQS) app (which I highly recommend). Using the DQS app, you focus less on a specific macronutrient (carbs, fats, proteins) or food type and more on simply whether the foods you eat are of high quality or low quality. You don't have to do a wholesale change in what you eat, like most "diets" force you to do; instead, you simply adjust your current diet to include more high-quality foods and fewer low-quality foods.

Instantly, your nutrition and running will be better. Simple as that. No more confusion on which food is the "best food for runners." Because guess what? There isn't one food or one type of food that is "best." I've had meals with Japanese Olympic runners, I've shared the table with Italian Olympic runners, and I've lived and eaten with Kenyan Olympic runners. At every table, the food eaten was very, very different. But every meal was of high quality, close to the earth (i.e., not highly processed), and varied.

The foods were also representative of the ingredients available to their local environment and were part of their culture. That's where we often go wrong: We force an unsustainable diet instead of simply cleaning up our current diet. A big change in diet (or types or preparation of foods) is often not sustainable. But improving the quality of what you already eat little by little is very sustainable.

Here are a few examples of how to raise the quality of foods by swapping lower-quality foods for higher-quality choices:

Lower-quality food	Higher-quality substitute
Diet soda	Seltzer water
French fries	Baked potato
Cereal and milk	Old-fashioned oatmeal with raisins and almond slivers
Energy bar	Whole-grain toast with natural (no-sugar-added) peanut butter
Frozen yogurt	Plain full-fat yogurt with fresh berries and a drizzle of honey

Remember that these are general guidelines; you need to figure out what works for you and your body. For instance, three women in a group of elite runners I coached learned they were sensitive to gluten (one even had celiac disease). Now gluten itself is not inherently good or bad; it's simply a protein in wheat—which, as a whole grain, is perfectly healthy for many runners! For these three women, however, when they eliminated gluten from their diets, the quality of their diet went way up. After all, gluten is prevalent in many low-quality foods. As they removed those low-quality foods, the women quickly felt and performed better, and our women's team went on to win the National Cross-Country Championship.

Again, I'm not saying you ought to be gluten-free. I'm just using this as an example to show that even among those striving for a high-quality diet, every runner is not the same. You don't have to abandon the foods that you like and that are an integral part of your culture and household. You just need to raise the quality of the foods you eat and be aware of how your body responds.

To get you started on what a healthy, high-quality diet looks like, here are some sample meal plans from Matt Fitzgerald. I use these with my runners and suggest you give them a try to see how easy and satisfying it is to eat a healthy runner's diet.

Morning-Run Day

Follow this meal plan if you run in the morning.

Meal	What to Eat
Pre-Run Snack	Banana
Breakfast	Vegetable frittata*
Lunch	Tuna salad sandwich: Tuna mixed with mashed avocado and diced sweet onion, lettuce, tomato, whole-grain bread
Optional Snack	Baby carrots with sugar-free peanut butter
Dinner	Turkey and cornbread "one bowl"* Garden salad with vinaigrette dressing
Dessert	Whole-milk Greek yogurt with raspberries and honey

*Recipes:

Vegetable Frittata: *Racing Weight Cookbook*, page 179

Turkey and cornbread "one bowl": *The Endurance Diet*, page 229

Afternoon-Run Day

Follow this meal plan if you run in the afternoon.

Meal	What to Eat
Breakfast	Low-sugar whole-grain granola Whole milk Raisins
Optional Snack	Raw cashews
Lunch	Chicken burrito: Corn tortilla, shredded grilled chicken, black beans, grilled green bell pepper and onions, mashed avocado, salsa Apple Dark chocolate
Pre-Run Snack	Banana
Dinner	Cashew-crusted salmon* Brown rice Steamed snow peas, lightly buttered
Dessert	Oatmeal and dried cranberry cookie

*Recipes:

Cashew-crusted salmon: *Racing Weight Cookbook*, page 151

Recovery/Non-Run Day

For those days when your runs are short and easy or you are taking the day off, follow this meal plan.

Meal	What to Eat
Breakfast	Broccoli cheese omelet*
Optional Snack	Raw cashews
Lunch	Cauliflower, white bean, and cheddar soup* Apple
Optional Snack	Soy protein shake
Dinner	Seared tuna with mango-cucumber salsa*
Dessert	Fresh raspberries with whole-milk low-sugar Greek yogurt

*Recipes:

Broccoli cheese omelet: *Racing Weight Cookbook*, page 107

Cauliflower, white bean, and cheddar soup: *Racing Weight Cookbook*, page 84

Seared tuna with mango-cucumber salsa: *Racing Weight Cookbook*, page 228

Lesson #30: Eat the Rainbow

A lesson I learned from top sports dietician Amanda Carlson-Phillips is to "eat the rainbow." If you look at most high-quality diet foods, they are a myriad of colors. When you include more vegetables and fruits as well as high-quality protein sources like salmon, your plate starts to look beautiful. It has lots of colors that look like what you'd find in nature.

Beyond being pretty, different colored foods (natural colors mind you, not artificial colors) also provide unique properties. You may have heard that eating carrots can help improve your vision. That's because carrots have beta-carotene, which turns them orange and is what the body uses to make Vitamin A—and Vitamin A plays a role in improving your vision. Another example is green leafy vegetables: They are great sources of iron, which runners need to carry oxygen to working muscles. And how about pineapple? It contains bromelain, which helps repair your muscles after a hard run.

So, eat the rainbow. This goes hand in hand with a high-quality diet and portion control, because you can only fit so much on your plate, so the more colors you have, the more manageable those portions become. Plus, it's hard to overeat a high-quality diet—natural, unprocessed, and varied foods satiate your hunger and fill your stomach, both of which keep you from overeating.

Contrast this with processed foods, which are designed to make you always want more. That's right, food scientists have concocted junk foods that actually make you crave more, ignore your body's normal fullness signals, and consume more and more of the low-quality foods. As a result, it's even more important to eat as many natural, unprocessed, "straight-from-the-earth" foods as you can so that there really isn't room in your diet for these addictive junk foods.

Coach Q&A: What about carbs, fats, and protein?

You'll notice that I didn't start our discussion of nutrition by diving straight into the macronutrients: carbohydrates, fats, and protein. Instead, I focused on improving the quality of your diet and eating a variety of foods. Again, that is because I think it's more sustainable for runners to concentrate on the quality and quantity of their foods than to worry about exact percentages of carbs, fats, and protein.

To be honest, I think talking about macronutrients pulls the runner off target. If you eat a clean diet with lots of colors and variety, you'll get all the carbs, fats, and protein you need. And guess what? Your body is smart. If it needs more of a macronutrient, you'll begin to crave it. Women sometimes experience this—they'll finish their menstrual cycle and crave

211

red meat. That's the body's intelligence: It knows she needs to replace iron that was lost, and red meat is full of iron.

If you simply pay attention to how you feel and adjust based off of that, you'll always have the right amount of carbs, fats, and protein. Feeling sore? Increase protein. Getting depleted on your long runs? Increase your carbohydrates. Find yourself constantly hungry even though you've been eating? Add more fat to your diet and you'll be satiated. Just remember to pay attention, and your body will tell you what you need.

Lesson #31: Stop Reward Eating

Runners often convince themselves that they've "earned" more food, especially unhealthy food, just because they ran. This is flawed reasoning. You don't see professionals downing chicken fingers and ice cream sundaes after every workout—and they're running more than most of us will ever run! That's because they know the importance of a consistently healthy diet and the difference it makes in performance. The same holds true for us recreational runners.

A treat every once in a while is totally fine, but don't buy into the "because I worked out I can eat whatever I want" fallacy.

I saw this flawed reasoning take hold firsthand in the first charity marathon group that I coached. Most of the athletes were out of shape and using the marathon as a way to get in shape, lose weight, and support a charity.

After our long runs—as many runners do—we'd all go to breakfast to refuel. After a few such breakfasts, I began to grow concerned. My runners were gorging themselves after their long runs, and this was counter to their goals.

As a result, I introduced the ideas of diet quality and eating the rainbow, as well as an understanding that a small reward is fine but that we all need to be careful not to overdo it. Soon, they began to see the rewards of a fitter, faster body and learned that a small treat is all one needs to feel the mental boost we deserve for working hard toward our goals.

Lesson #32: Adjust Carbs for Training & Racing

The basic eating patterns we just described will get you through all manner of easy runs, so long as those runs don't last too long (my rule of thumb is 90 minutes or less). Occasionally, however, you might perform a longer and/or more intense workout. For these workouts you want full carbohydrate stores, meaning you want your glycogen (that is, the carbohydrates your body stores in your muscles for fuel) as stocked up as your body will allow. To do this, you need to adapt your diet so that you eat more carbs—and absorb them—in advance of the workout.

Now what this *doesn't* mean is that you should overeat. You aren't "stuffing yourself" to get fuller glycogen stores, and you certainly aren't upping your carb intake all the time. This is a mistake I see a lot of beginner marathoners make. They've heard they need to eat lots of carbs, so they add more pasta, rice, and starches to their diet. Then, they've also heard that they need sports drinks and energy gels during their runs, so they add those too.

However, all of that advice is based off of research on world-class runners conducted back in the late 1960s and through the 1970s. These elite runners ran 80–150 miles per week. They burned a lot of carbohydrates running all of those miles (including the two to three fast workouts within the week), so naturally they needed lots of carbohydrates. The prevailing wisdom that emerged was that all runners needed to eat lots of carbohydrates, but this concept is flawed.

Beginning marathoners run much lower mileage, so they have plenty of stored carbohydrate (glycogen) from their regular diet. If they eat the same diet as an elite athlete, they'll wind up consuming excess calories, which will be converted to fat.

The point is that the "Eat like an elite" concept isn't literal, just like the "Train like an elite" concept isn't literal. It means to take the concepts that successful runners have and modify them for your situation. So, if you are just doing a short, low-intensity run, you have plenty of carbohydrates already in your body to fuel this run. You don't need extra carbohydrates in your diet to restock your stores, because you haven't burned through them. Just eat a high-quality, well-balanced diet like we described in *Lesson #29: Focus on Diet Quality*, and you'll have all of the fuel you need.

However, if you do a long run or a hard workout, then you want to make sure your carbohydrate stores are fully stocked, and, because you'll burn through them during the run, you'll need to replenish them afterwards. As a result, non-elite runners need to modulate their carbohydrate intake around their hard and/or long workouts but otherwise keep carbohydrate intake more in balance.

Here's how this might look for a non-elite runner who runs four days per week with one quality workout and a long run:

Day	Run	Diet
Monday	Easy Run	Normal
Tuesday	OFF or Cross-train	Normal but with extra carbs at dinner to prepare for tomorrow's speed workout
Wednesday	Speed Workout	Extra carbs in first meal after speed workout, then normal
Thursday	Easy Run	Normal
Friday	OFF or Cross-train	Normal but with extra carbs at dinner to prepare for tomorrow's long run
Saturday	Long Run	Extra carbs in first meal after long run, then normal
Sunday	OFF	Normal

My experience helping lots of adult runners who don't run mega-miles but are trying to get fast and stay lean is that this modulation of carbohydrates is key. You don't have to go carb-free on non-key workout days, but you don't add extra carbs when you don't need them. In other words, you only "carb up" around your hard and/or long workouts.

Here's a more specific example: Let's say you have a fast finish long run coming up on Saturday morning. Sometime between Thursday and Friday morning (12–24 hours before the workout) you should start being more mindful of the carb component of your regular meals. If, for instance, you usually have a smoothie with protein powder for breakfast, maybe use UCAN or another slow-release carbohydrate source instead of protein powder to up the carb component. Or if you have a salad with chicken for lunch, maybe swap in rice for some or all of the salad. There's no need to go crazy shoveling platefuls of pasta and garlic bread down the hatch; you're just mindfully ensuring that your glycogen stores get topped up in time to give you the best chance to make the most of your workout.

One final perk of this carb modulation regimen is that you can use it as a dress rehearsal for how you plan to eat leading up to your big race. By trying out different foods and meals now, you'll figure out what gives you sustained energy versus what might upset your stomach. It's certainly better to find out in training than on race day!

Lesson #33: Eat to Recover

We've said a lot about fueling to run. Now it's time to talk about a much-neglected part of runner nutrition: fueling to *recover* from all that running.

How Your Muscles Recover

When you run, and especially when you run fast and/or for a long time, your body burns onboard fuel. Specifically, you burn through your carbohydrate stores: glucose (in the blood) and glycogen (in the muscles). Afterwards, your ability to recover in time for your next workout is heavily impacted by your muscles' ability to restock their glycogen stores.

Fortunately, your body knows this and tries to help you out. Right after a workout—within the first 30 minutes in particular, and within 2 hours generally—your system is primed to restock glycogen. Specifically, the hormone that tells your body to convert carbohydrates to glycogen, insulin, ramps that process up to 300% of its normal rate. Therefore, if you eat carbs post-run, a bunch of extra glycogen gets made and quickly socked away in your muscles.

Interestingly, scientists have found that ingesting protein along with carbohydrates increases your insulin response. As a result, you can store up to 30% more glycogen if you eat a protein-and-carbohydrate combination after your run than if you eat carbs alone. Plus, the protein helps with recovery, specifically with rebuilding tissues that may have been damaged while you exercised.

There's been a fair amount of research suggesting various "optimal ratios" of carbohydrate to protein—somewhere in the range of 2:1 to 4:1 grams of carbohydrates to protein. Realistically, all you need to worry about is having a little protein with whatever carbohydrate you're ingesting. I find liquids are often easiest for athletes to consume after a hard workout, so you can buy or make a quick shake with juice, frozen fruit, and a scoop of peanut butter or other protein source. If you're in a rush, even something like SlimFast will work!

In sum, by eating a carb-and-protein snack within 30 minutes of your workout, you feed the system that is trying to restock the carbohydrates you just used and jumpstart your body's ability to recover for your next workout. What's more, eating soon after you work out helps you feel more satiated so that when you are ready to sit down to a larger meal a little later (ideally within 2 hours of your workout), you don't succumb as easily to reward eating and instead can make higher-quality food choices due to the fact that you're not starving.

Create Your Nutritional Recovery Routine

So now let's create a nutritional recovery routine for you. Start by aiming to eat one gram of carbohydrate for every pound of body weight in the first 2 hours following your workout, and match this with the appropriate ratio of protein. For example, if you weigh 100 pounds, then you need 100 grams of carbohydrate and 25 grams of protein (following the 4 grams carb to 1 gram protein ratio). If you weigh 160 pounds, then you need 160 grams of carbohydrate and 40 grams of protein. Admittedly, that's a lot of carbohydrate, which is why this routine is just for after your very hard and/or long workouts and races.

Because the greatest recovery period happens within the first half hour, I've found that aiming to ingest half of your carbohydrate needs in that timeframe is ideal. For our 100-pound runner, eating 50 grams of carbohydrates (and the accompanying 13 grams of protein) in that timeframe might be a real challenge, so I encourage athletes to make a recovery shake instead of trying to force down solid food. Then you can shower and take care of other life things before following with a full, healthy meal containing a base of carbohydrates and some protein (e.g., pasta and meat, rice and fish, or pancakes and eggs).

Lastly, don't forget: You'll also need to rehydrate! I recommend drinking a half liter to a liter of fluids every hour until you're urinating once per hour and your urine is straw-colored.

Quick Recap: Refueling

Here are some quick numbers to summarize how to refuel properly after your hard workouts and long runs:

- Eat within **30 minutes** of finishing
- Consume **1 gram of carb** for every 1 pound of body weight
- Include protein, based on **2:1 to 1:4 carbs-to-protein ratio**
- Drink **0.5–1 liter fluid/hour** until rehydrated

Lesson #34: Losing Weight While Training

Before I go into this final nutrition topic, I want to make something clear: This is a book about running. It's not a book about weight loss. Therefore, when it comes to runner nutrition, *weight loss is icing, not cake.* And in many cases, it's entirely unnecessary.

If you've implemented all the guidance I've offered up to this point, then ask yourself: Is my body staying healthy and doing what I'm asking of it? Am I making improvements in my running? If so, I'd argue that you don't need to focus on losing weight. If you have excess pounds to shed, your body will do that naturally, without any interference on your part. And if you're not losing weight, you very well might already be at your optimal performance weight. Remember, that's what we're focused on here: performance.

To this point, I want to add that "heavier" doesn't always equal "slower." (I've seen some women come back from pregnancy 5 or 10 pounds heavier and run better than ever!) Also make sure you look at body composition before you start trying to lose weight, because you may be dealing with muscle, not fat, and that muscle is what's helping you to run fast, so you certainly don't want to lose it.

All of that being said, if you do have some extra weight you want to lose, try to lose it before you get into serious training. The best time to start modifying your diet is during the off-season or during a base-building phase so you don't risk compromising your race-specific running training.

The next thing to note is that weight loss is a very, very gradual process. You can really only lose about 0.5 to 1 pound of weight per week without compromising your running training. Plus, the healthier your diet becomes and the closer you get to your optimal performance weight, the more slowly the weight loss will happen. Again, I really encourage you to focus on how you are feeling and performing—if you're making fitness gains, staying injury free, and feeling good, you probably don't need to worry about those "last few pounds." Numbers on a scale are just that: numbers on a scale.

With all of that in mind, here are a few basic strategies that I've seen work with athletes I've coached:

Eliminate mindless eating. Look for the times and places where you most often fall into this trap, and (1) eliminate the food from the situation (you don't need ice cream to watch television at night), (2) eliminate the distraction (don't scroll through social media while eating breakfast), or (3) change the setting (take your lunch and any snacks to the cafeteria rather than eating at your desk).

Make sure to hydrate between and before meals. Try drinking a glass of water first when you get the urge to snack between meals and also before meals. You'll be less likely to overeat, and you'll improve your hydration.

Beware liquid calories. Many common drinks like sodas, sports drinks, and juices are highly caloric, and most of these calories are from fast-acting sugars. Overconsuming carbohydrates—especially fast-acting sugars—when you don't need them results in fat storage. So be intentional about when you choose these beverages over a simple glass of water.

Eat your veggies first. When you sit down to a meal, start with a salad or whatever vegetable is on your plate. This can help improve your diet quality score at the outset of the meal and, if you're feeling ravenous, helps to fill you up a bit before you move on to more calorically dense foods.

Use your hand to measure portions. These days, we have so much food available at all times and in such huge quantities that the idea of a "portion" can get all out of whack. Registered Dietician Amanda Carlson-Phillips suggests using your hand to determine portion sizes as follows:

226

Be realistic about your snacking. Snacking is okay, as long as it is intentional. If you're snacking a lot, counterbalance with smaller meals, and, within those meals, focus on foods that are higher in protein and fat, which will help you feel satiated.

I cannot emphasize enough how tangential weight loss is to running. People talk about making "race weight," but in my opinion, your race weight is whatever weight enables you to run fast and stay healthy and injury free. When it comes to nutrition, your primary goal should always be your health, and if you're making healthy choices with every meal, then don't worry too much about weight—your body will get to where it needs to be!

BRAIN TRAINING

It's 100% Mental

We've talked about run training, injury prevention, running form, and nutrition. These all help us to train bodies, which are indeed very important for running and racing. However, we have yet to address an equally important aspect we need to train: our minds.

In my opinion, we talk too much about the physical part of running and too little about the mental side. Because it's the mental side where most of the training and racing happen. Yes, you must be physically fit, but your mind is what chooses to get out for your run or not, to keep pushing even when the fatigue messages are growing louder, and to race competitors and the clock to attempt a win or a personal best.

With that in mind, let's discuss some key brain training lessons.

Lesson #35: Maintaining Motivation

Every experienced runner knows that running success ultimately comes down to simply lacing up the shoes and getting out the door. At times, this is easy. The weather is great. You feel like a million bucks. Your life stress is low, and you're meeting up with your running friends. At other times, you have zero motivation to get out the door, even though you know you should. That's where "brain training" is key.

When working with runners, I not only help them accept that motivation will vary (and that variance is perfectly normal), but I also help them develop strategies to minimize low motivation and deal with it when it happens. Here's how:

First, look across your training and think about when you are uber-motivated. What is the scenario? For me, it's when I'm consistent in my training; when I get out first thing in the morning; when the weather is warm and sunny; and, maybe most importantly, when I'm meeting someone and we're training for a big race.

On the flip side, injuries, life stress, missing the run early in the day, and cold weather are my nemeses. When any of these happen, I'm at a high risk of missing my run, because my motivation gets low.

What about you? Write down the conditions when you are motivated and when you aren't. (Don't be lazy—actually write them down!) This gives you your blueprint for what works and what doesn't, which will make the next part easier.

Now you need to develop strategies for weathering the low motivation times and for building confidence through consistency and fewer "bad" workouts. Here are some that work really well for everyone from new runners to Olympians.

1. Get on a plan (and choose the right one).

Remember *Lesson #11: Picking the Right Plan*? You learned how to choose the plan that will work best for you. Maintaining motivation is a big part of why picking the right plan is so important.

Smart training plans are designed for success. They are set up so that you are highly likely to complete the workouts and feel good about them. This boosts your motivation, because when training is going well consistently over time, runners are always more motivated.

(To take it to the next level with an added dose of accountability, consider hiring a coach as well.)

2. Set some goals.

Goal setting, which we talked about in *Lesson #10: Setting Your Goal*, is another way to stay motivated. Goals help to get you out the door, because they give you a very concrete "why."

My wife is a runner who requires goals. Whereas I run no matter if I have a big race coming up or not, she needs the big goal; otherwise, she's apt to miss a few runs, then a few more, and soon, she's out of shape and starting over (which she hates). To combat this, she always keeps a big goal on the calendar—something a little scary so she's sure to get out the door.

Remember earlier, when I mentioned that she recently used a 30K trail race for just this purpose? Her running had been hit or miss, so she signed up for the race and instantly had new motivation for training. The racecourse was quite challenging, and she knew she wouldn't finish without adequate preparation, which helped her stay motivated and consistent. She ended up having a great race.

If you battle inconsistency and lose motivation frequently, consider a robust racing calendar to keep you engaged in your running.

3. Get a buddy (in person or online).

The buddy system is an excellent way to maintain motivation and get yourself out the door when you really don't want to. Whether it's an in-person training partner or group or an online running system like the McMillan Run Team, accountability to others helps you stay motivated. Plus, when you're running with someone, the miles go by faster, and the shared suffering creates a bond that will help keep you going when motivation is low. I highly recommend a running buddy or system.

4. Prioritize running in your weekly calendar.

One motivation- and consistency-killer is our modern-day life schedule. With work, family, and other commitments competing for your limited time, it can be easy to miss runs and lose motivation. To combat this, I suggest you prioritize your running first in your weekly calendar. This might sound selfish on the surface, but I bet you would agree that you are a better spouse, parent, coworker, boss, and citizen when you make time to run regularly. So look ahead each week and pre-plan around potential issues that could derail your run. Your body, mind, family, and community will be better for it.

5. When all else fails, default to discipline.

Sometimes, in spite of the best planning, you really just don't want to go run. That's when you need to default to discipline. On these low-motivation days, just getting out the door is a big win. No matter what happens, you can be proud of yourself for not giving in to the temptation to skip your run.

That said, you'll often find that getting out the door is the hardest part; the run usually goes just fine after that! But even if it doesn't and you only manage 5–10 minutes of running, I still encourage you to call it a win. The more you can will yourself to lace 'em up and go, the more practice your brain gets and the easier it tends to become. On these days, any running is good running, and the pride you feel pays big dividends to motivation and consistency.

I'll finish by admitting that these five strategies are easy to say but sometimes hard to do. At the end of the day, just realize that even if you have a period of low motivation or miss a few runs, all is not lost. Simply "get back on the horse," as they say, and start up again. Just like running takes practice to improve, these mental strategies take practice too!

Lesson #36: Keep an Awesomeness Journal

Our brains have an inherent negative bias. There is an entire subdiscipline of neuroscience devoted to this subject, but what we as runners need to know is that our negative bias is why we dwell longer and more intensely on something negative compared to something positive. You have probably experienced this. Ten people might compliment you on your new hairstyle, but if one person says something negative, you think more about the negative comment, don't you?

The same goes for running: You can have ten good runs, but as soon as you have a bad run, you dwell on that one. Doing so erodes your confidence and challenges your motivation. To combat this, I recommend all runners to keep an Awesomeness Journal.

An Awesomeness Journal is a collection of runs, workouts, and races where you showed your awesomeness. It can also include motivational quotes, inspirational photos, or anything that reminds you that you are, indeed, awesome.

Think back across the last few months. Remember a handful of runs where you felt fantastic? Or what about times when you didn't want to run, but you did anyway? That's what you put in your Awesomeness Journal.

Then, when you start to feel down or doubt yourself, pull out your Awesomeness Journal and read through it. See? You are awesome! Your negative bias is just messing with you. You don't even have to "fake it till you make it"—you've already proven your awesomeness time and time again. The journal is your reminder.

Lesson #37: Seeking Suffering

This brain training lesson results in the most unusual looks from runners. After all, aren't we usually trying to avoid suffering? Well, in running, you actually have to seek it out in order to be your best. The reason is due to how our brains work.

According to one theory of the brain called the "central governor model," the brain is set up to protect you from danger. Your brain is constantly monitoring your body, and if it senses something concerning, it begins a process to protect itself. In running, a big part of that process involves sending fatigue messages to your mind. (It's even proposed that your brain can cut the power to your working muscles as well.)

An example for the new runner is when you go for those first few runs: Your breathing is heavy, your muscles are uncoordinated, and your heart rate is high as your body tries desperately to get the working muscles to do what you're asking. Your brain sees all of this as a big threat to your normal status, so it sends lots and lots of fatigue messages to your mind. That's why those first runs are so tough: Not only are you not yet physically trained for them, but your brain is screaming at you to stop.

After a few runs, however, your body starts to adapt—your breathing is more under control and you feel smoother. Most importantly, your brain no longer views running as a threat, so you now have to run faster and/or longer before it sends the same amount of fatigue messages as on those earlier runs.

The trick in training, then, is to gradually yet steadily provide the brain with a little more suffering and a little more suffering. Done across a training cycle, you can get to where you can endure a very high level of suffering without giving in to the fatiguing messages. This is where your breakthrough performances come.

I should note that many runners use the term "pain" when talking about mental suffering, but I prefer "suffering." I've seen too many new runners run through physical pain and injury because they heard a pro runner say that she endured "painful" workouts that helped her to achieve best

242

performance. Do not run through physical pain. Mental pain (aka suffering) is what we're talking about.

So just how do you do this? The drip method. A little bit of suffering done frequently, with the occasional big exposure, not only gets you physically ready but gets you mentally ready for the demands of the race.

A smart training plan provides one to three workouts per week where you seek out a little bit of suffering. The suffering can come from the speed of the run, the duration, or both. In these workouts, you are forced to combat the fatigue/"stop" messages in order to keep going. If you've chosen your plan wisely, the suffering is at an appropriate level, and in most instances you can push through. If you can just keep pushing when you're tired, you give yourself a great chance at success.

This leads us to another key aspect of brain training: mantra development. When combating suffering, you must find a way to stay on task and avoid giving in to the fatiguing messages of the brain. Most runners develop mantras or thought patterns to accomplish this. For some, it's as easy as a simple statement like

243

"Stay strong" or "You can do it." For others, they use physical cues like shaking out their arms or focusing on their running form to keep them going despite the fatigue.

Key workouts provide ideal opportunities to determine the best mental strategy that keeps you on pace. You'll want to have this in your arsenal for your race.

Lastly, when you build your tolerance for mental suffering in this gradual yet progressive way, it builds your confidence. If you suffer too much (by training too hard too soon), you'll give in to the suffering and have a bad workout, which erodes your confidence (thanks to that pesky negative bias!). Not so when done correctly. If you have brain training as part of your objective for these key workouts and you train at the right level, then you feel great about yourself after the workout, and that builds confidence that you can achieve your goal. (More on this later.)

The take-home message is that to be the best runner you can be, you must seek suffering. Don't do it on every run, but instead use your key workouts as a chance to challenge yourself physically and mentally, so you develop the mental fortitude you'll need for your race. Viewing suffering as a goal of a workout will help you to get more out of yourself, and even on those days when things aren't going well, you'll see the value in the "bad workout"—they still provide a hefty dose of brain training.

Lesson #38: Go Zone to Race Your Best

Going into races, runners put a lot of thought into their pacing and fueling strategies. But very few runners plan how they want to think during a race.

That's right: You need to think about how you want to think. What thoughts do you want to have in the early part of the race? What about in the middle? What about during that big climb at mile four? And how will you think if your pacing isn't going according to plan?

For many runners, this is a new idea, and it might sound like a crazy one, but I'm telling you, it works great. And that's because your optimal mindset must vary across the race. Plus, things don't always go according to plan, so you need to have contingency plans to manage your mind when things go awry.

Many years ago, I wrote an article for *Running Times* magazine on the Go Zone Racing Method. This is my general thinking plan for racing. To this day, I still hear from runners across the globe who read the article and used the Go Zone mindset to finally break through and run the race they always knew they could.

Here's how it goes:

Go Zone racing involves serious mental toughness and some risk-taking, as well as a heavy dose of prerace planning. It is not for the faint of heart. It is for runners who want to challenge themselves to go beyond their previous bests.

In short, Go Zone racing puts particular emphasis on the most critical race stage—the stage where you are most likely to let your pace, and your goal, slip away. For most runners, this occurs in the third quarter of races. However, with the right mindset, you'll turn this into your Go Zone and your next races into breakthroughs.

Prerace

In the hours (and possibly days) leading up to the race, get mentally ready to run fast. The efficacy of this is demonstrated in the "Carlsbad Phenomenon." The Carlsbad 5000 in California is the site of multiple world records and untold PRs by inspired non-elite runners. These records are not because the course is fast. In fact, the course includes two 90-degree turns and two 180-degree turns, plus two slight inclines. So, while it's not the toughest course in the world, it also doesn't seem especially conducive to running super-fast.

The answer? It's the mindset. Everyone knows the race is going to be fast, so they get mentally ready for it. They expect it to be a fast race, and so it is.

Transfer the Carlsbad Phenomenon to your next race. Go into it expecting it to be fast, and it likely will be.

The Start

In the Start Zone, you must be mentally focused on your objective. In shorter races like a 5K, your mind must be ready to get going quickly but under control. Since the start of a race can feel chaotic, it's important that you don't get distracted by others and instead know exactly how you want to approach the first few minutes of the race.

For longer races like the half- and full marathon, the mental plan at the start has to be to hold yourself back. You want to keep your effort controlled, even if it feels like you could go faster, because you'll need all of your energy for later in the race.

No matter what type of race you are running, the point is that you need a mental plan for the start. Know ahead of time what thoughts you are going to rely on to achieve your best in that section of the race.

Once you've run some races, you'll learn your most common errors/mistakes and can then tweak your plan to avoid these and give yourself the best chance for a great performance.

Fast Rhythm Zone

The next section of the race, after the flurry of the start and up until halfway, is about finding a relaxed but fast rhythm—that cadence and stride that are quick but relaxed and where you are smooth and fast. You are simply trying to stay on pace but cover ground as easily as possible. If you can do this and do it relatively relaxed, you'll be ready to attack the Go Zone.

The Go Zone

This is it! After you pass through the halfway point, you enter the Go Zone. In this section, the race will be getting harder and harder, so you must increase your intensity to keep the pace going. Think of this as the time to "attack" the race.

In addition to increasing your intensity internally here, it can be useful to focus on something external as well. If racing in a pack, move up in the group. If racing in a line of runners, pass someone. If racing alone, pick out a point up ahead on the road or track and focus on running harder to that point. Then, pick another point or pass another person. Do whatever you must to keep the pace going. There will be suffering—breakthroughs always require suffering—but if you can just push harder here to keep your pace on target, you will achieve your goal.

I cannot overstate this: The Go Zone is where you should spend the majority of your effort mentally preparing. Get ready for it. Make a plan. Know the mantras and mentality you are going to use, and then commit to them. The first few times, it's scary, but soon you learn that the Go Zone is where the magic happens and virtually guarantees that you will be satisfied with your race.

The Get-Time Zone

Once through the third quarter of a race, you enter the Get-Time Zone. We can all sprint faster than our goal pace "right at the end"—the key is that you must start your push earlier than you normally do. Don't wait until you see the finish line; the last hundred meters is too close to score many precious seconds. If you start your push to the line earlier (with 1 to 2 minutes to go in a 5K or 10K race, for example), you'll shave off several seconds that can be the difference between a PR and a disappointment. It's not easy, of course, but if you can get your brain to risk it and your legs to obey, you can Get Time.

Even in longer races, the Get-Time Zone offers huge opportunities. I've definitely had marathons where I gave in to the pity party in the last few miles and shortly after finishing looked back and knew I had plenty of chances to run faster. Plus, since the pace can slow more significantly in longer races than in shorter races, the Get-Time Zone offers a great chance to gain a lot of time.

It might take several races before you get the hang of Go Zone racing, but try it enough and eventually it will become the norm. In fact, you can get in even more practice by using the Go Zone in workouts. Mentally break your workouts in half, and think of the second half as the Go Zone time. Challenge yourself to up your intensity and mental focus in the Go Zone, workout after workout. This repetition engrains the Go Zone mentality until it becomes second nature. Your workouts and your racing will yield the benefits. Plus, most of us don't preplan how we want to think. We preplan pacing but not our mentality, which we leave to chance. Don't do that anymore. Think about how you want to think.

If your experience is like that of others who have mastered the Go Zone, get ready to rewrite your personal record book.

Prerace	Prepare your mind for what to expect
Start *(first half)*	Focus on your early-race objective (go out strong, hold back, etc.)
Go Zone *(third quarter)*	Increase intensity, find a point of focus, and attack the race
Get-Time Zone *(final quarter)*	Push to the finish line faster than goal pace

Coach Q&A: Should I use the Go Zone method for every single race?

Not necessarily. For example, if you try to use the Go Zone method in a race early in your season when you aren't yet fit enough, you'll probably wind up frustrated when you try to kick at the end of the race and your body simply cannot respond.

Therefore, I have created five **Go Zone Racing Rules** to help guide you on how and when to implement this method.

1. You should practice the Go Zone in your workouts so you are ready when it comes time to race.

2. You must be race fit. For that reason, Go Zone tactics work well later in the race season.

3. You must be realistic in your racing goal relative to your training. No wishful thinking or exaggerating what is possible.

4. You must be willing to straddle the fine line between going too fast and going perfectly fast. Even "failure" will help you better understand where that line is.

5. You must be engaged in your races and specifically focus on the task of each zone.

Lesson #39: Free Speed

You might be wondering why there is a chapter in the Brain Training section called "free speed." After all, speed comes from fitness, and fitness comes from the body, right?

Wrong!

Well, you're partially right. You do need physical fitness to run fast. But most athletes don't run to their maximum physical fitness. Ask any high school coach. She'll tell you that the kids are fit, but until she can "flip the switch" and get them excited about testing their limits, taking chances, and really pushing themselves in the final few minutes of the race, they never run as fast as they are capable of running.

However, when a young runner does put herself out there, she runs to her potential. She gets free speed, in that she didn't have to increase her fitness at all, she just needed to have the right mindset and voila, she runs 5–10 seconds faster per mile. That's why I call this "free speed"—without training harder, you actually *can* run faster. The brain is that powerful.

254

Adult runners are similar, and that's why the Go Zone Method leads to so many breakthroughs. These runners aren't necessarily any fitter, but once they actually push themselves, they run faster—free speed.

Not convinced of the power of the mind? In 1988, German social psychologist Fritz Strack and colleagues published research on "smiling." In the experiment, subjects were asked to look at cartoons and rate how funny they were. One group of subjects was told to hold a pencil in their lips without letting it touch their teeth (the "frowning" group), another group was instructed to hold the pencil with their teeth so it didn't touch their lips (the "smiling" group), and a third group held the pencil in their hands. Lo and behold, the subjects holding the pencil between their lips ("frowning") thought the cartoons were less funny than the subjects with the pencil in their hand, while the "smiling" group thought the cartoons were the funniest. Ergo, a few simple facial muscle contractions can change how we perceive things.

Be open to your own greatness and start to look for opportunities for free speed. They usually happen when you are engaged in your workouts or races. Get engaged mentally, use the Go Zone, and I guarantee you'll run faster without any changes in physical fitness.

Lesson #40: Personality Type & Tendencies

Every runner has tendencies, or ways we tend to think, which then inform our actions. Some runners have a tendency to overtrain. Others have tendencies to beat themselves up over a missed workout or to skip rehab. A lot of coaching, in fact, is about identifying tendencies in an athlete and then creating strategies to capitalize on the positive ones (and yes, there are positive ones!) and eliminate or at least reduce the negative ones. So that's what we're going to do here: help you identify your own tendencies and then come up with ways you can harness the good and banish the bad.

Personality Informs Tendencies

Identifying personality type is a "broad stroke" way to capture a whole host of tendencies you might have and help you get a head start on making the best of what you've got.

The most well-known personality research comes from the 1950s and categorizes people into Type A and Type B personalities. This is not better or worse than the myriad of other personality research out there, but it is some of the simplest and most familiar, so it's what I often use when I am first getting to know an athlete. The thing to recognize with the Type A/B categorization is that these are extreme characterizations and don't apply to all situations; you can be Type A in one part of your life and Type B in another.

Here are some broad definitions of the two types:

Type A: outgoing, ambitious, extremely organized, status-conscious, sensitive, impatient, anxious, proactive, "workaholics," hate delays and ambivalence

Type B: lower stress levels, work steadily, care more about the journey than the outcome, reflective, relaxed

Does one type sound better to you than the other? Well don't be fooled. Neither is better or worse; they both have their tendencies, good and bad. Here's a very short list of some of the *negative* tendencies for each personality type:

Type A tendencies
Push too hard
Worry/obsess
Never satisfied
Hypercompetitive
Can be own worst enemy
Type B tendencies
Delay/procrastinate
Skip or reduce
Too relaxed
At risk for lack of preparation
Too easily satisfied

Once you figure out your personality type, you can use some training tricks to turn type-based negative tendencies into strengths. For instance, when I start training a Type A athlete, I always make sure to build recovery blocks into their plan. This ensures that they will actually take that recovery time and feel good about it ("It's in the plan!"), rather than overtraining or feeling "lazy" when they take what is actually very necessary recovery. I also work hard to help them objectively review their workouts and races, because these runners tend to focus exclusively on the negative—even when the overall workout or race objectively went quite well!

On the other hand, if I'm training a Type B runner, I have to change my approach. Whereas I needed to help the Type A runner take a break once in a while, I need to try and motivate the Type B runner to adhere to the schedule I give them. This can include coaxing them to find a training partner (for accountability) or frequently reminding them of their goals (to generate excitement) and how the work they are doing will help them get there.

Common Negative Runner Tendencies

While each personality type has its strengths and weaknesses, it's the negative tendencies that hold us back. After coaching a wide range of runners for over thirty years, I've seen a lot of different negative tendencies block runners from achieving their goals. Here are some of the most common ones:

- Starting too fast in workouts
- Skipping prehab routines
- Not taking a proper rest period between training

cycles
- Poor snacking
- Negative self-talk
- Running too fast on easy days
- Giving up in races
- Dwelling on "bad" workouts
- Poor preparation/rushing fitness
- Ignoring aches/pains/tightness
- Overscheduling, particularly on key workout days and/or before big races

Do any of these sound like you? Let me offer a few real-life illustrations to help you see if you can relate.

Kelly the Mom

I coach a woman named Kelly. She's a dedicated and disciplined runner who, over the last couple of years, has dropped her marathon time from 3:52:37 to 3:21:48 and qualified for Boston. As you might expect, she has her sights set on a faster time in her next marathon (3:15:00), and I feel one of the keys will be overcoming her biggest negative tendency.

Kelly is a busy mom with three young kids. Her negative tendency is that toward the end of long runs and hard workouts, her mind shifts to getting back to her family, and as soon as she hits the door, she, like many moms, immediately focuses on everyone else. That, of course, is one of the greatest attributes of moms, but for Kelly, it means that after hard and/or long workouts, she often skips post-workout fueling.

As you read about in *Lesson #33: Eat to Recover,* Kelly's tendency to skip refueling after her runs means that her recovery is longer than it needs to be. This then means the quality of her next key session is compromised, and/or we have to delay it by an additional day or two because she's not recovered. Over time, repeating this pattern hurts the quality of her training. And since she's shooting for another big jump in performance, this makes a big difference.

Of course, this negative tendency is an easy one to overcome. The solution we developed is that before she does a hard workout or long run, Kelly prepares a recovery shake and has it at the ready, either in the car for runs away from home or in the fridge for runs that end at her house. She *must drink the shake* within 30 minutes of finishing her hard/long workout to take advantage of the enhanced recovery window. After just three weeks of the new strategy, we are seeing her recover faster, and the upcoming key workouts are of higher quality. Plus, she's gotten her kids involved: They help her make the shakes, and when she arrives home, they *all* take a break to have recovery drinks.

Alice the Pro

I also coach a professional runner named Alice. Her negative tendency is to start too fast in workouts. No matter how much I emphasize the proper pacing, she charges off and runs too fast. Naturally, this either leads us to shorten her workout (because she's so tired) or results in her bulling her way through the workout yet failing to get the stimulus we wanted. Often, this latter event compromises upcoming workouts, and I have to scramble because the training fatigue is greater than we'd planned.

To fix her tendency, I use two solutions. For short, fast repetitions (like 200-meter or 400-meter repeats on the track), I make her do "pace strides" before we start the workout. After her warm-up, I have her run 100 meters at the goal pace for the workout. It usually takes her three to four pace strides before she dials in the pace, and we can then begin the workout. The result is that she's better at hitting her goal pace after these pace strides without overshooting it.

For longer repeats (like 800-meter to 1-mile repeats), I have her run 1 mile at tempo pace. This seems to settle her down, and then she runs more controlled in the speed workout. These are simple yet effective solutions, and Alice has had big breakthroughs in training and racing since she's reduced this particular negative tendency.

Seth the Snacker

Seth is an age-group runner whose goal is to qualify for Boston. He works really hard, but his negative tendency is that he snacks too often and makes poor snacking decisions. To battle this tendency, our new rule is that he can still snack, but instead of grabbing the bag of chips or sleeve of cookies, he has to put his serving of the snack into a bowl.

By interrupting the "eat the whole bag" tendency, we're finding that Seth more easily controls the quantity of his snacking. Our next step is to transition to healthier snacks, but this negative tendency is really, really strong for Seth, so, we're taking it slow. Small victories lead to winning the battle.

Brent the Brain-Smasher

Brent is a driven runner (which is awesome) and very, very hard on himself (which is not). I get the feeling there may be some deeper psychological issues at play, but the manifestation is that he has a lot of negative self-talk. It's almost like he won't allow himself to achieve his goals. He may have a positive workout, but he won't bask in the glory of that. Instead, he seems to seek out any negative in the workout or himself and dwell on it.

With Brent, our solution is to develop a list of affirmations that he must read every day. Right now, it's forced: He's reading the positive self-statements but doesn't really believe them. However, having had experience with other athletes like Brent, I know that you can "fake it till you make it." And I'm seeing some cracks in the armor. He makes more positive statements after positive workouts and is expressing less general negativity. I have my fingers crossed that he'll be kinder to himself as time goes on. Psychologists tell us that the brain is very receptive to self-talk, so I'm hopeful that if we keep with it, we can reduce Brent's negative tendency.

What You Can Do

Take about a week to think about the negative tendencies that are hurting your running. Once you identify them, make a plan. Trust me, a small change in just one of your negative tendencies can make a huge difference in your training and racing.

Here's a concrete way to do this: Fold or draw a line down the center of a piece of paper. On one side, list your negative tendencies and the things that are holding you back from achieving your goals. Next, go back through your list and rank them in order of priority. Think about the ones that are easiest to overcome and/or will have the greatest impact if you can reduce them.

Then, on the other half of the paper, write down actions you could take to lessen, interrupt, or eliminate each negative tendency. For Kelly, one side says "skipping post-workout shake" and the other side says "recovery shake pre-made and ready post-workout." For Brent, one side says "negative self-talk" and the other side says "read daily affirmations aloud."

The last step in the exercise is to rip the page in half and dispose of the side with the negative tendencies. Post the side with the action items somewhere prominent so it will spur you to work on them.

And then give yourself time. It's not uncommon for a relapse to occur every now and then, but across a training cycle, I find that athletes really can change their tendencies. It's just about focusing on a new way of doing things—developing new habits and, as with physical training, building a new you.

Lesson #41: Prerace: Protect the Brain

It's fairly common knowledge that no training you do two weeks out from a marathon is going to improve your physical fitness prior to the race. However, those workouts could make or break your race based on what they do to another vitally important organ: your brain.

As we've discussed, your brain has an innate negative bias. Therefore, the key to prepping for the big race ahead is to boost your confidence and counter self-doubt. As a coach, that means helping an athlete avoid any workouts or situations where they might not have a positive result in the last two to three weeks leading up to a race. This doesn't mean I don't challenge my athletes in the month before the race, but I do look closely at their runner type and personality type and make sure that any workout I give them falls into their areas of strength so they can feel confident and nail it.

Sometimes this means forgoing the "better" workout. For instance, if I were just looking at the physical equation, I might really want to give a marathoner a tempo run seven to ten days before the marathon. But if this marathoner is a Type A Speedster who had a poor tempo run earlier in the training cycle, I'm going to skip it. It's too risky for her brain. Instead, I'll ask her what workout she loved and insert that one. I might modify the total volume of the workout, given that the race is coming up, but I know she's going to love the workout and that it will boost her confidence.

The bottom line is that when it comes time to race, hurting an athlete's confidence is worse than skipping any specific workout. So when your race is approaching, adjust, adjust, adjust! Do everything you can to protect your brain from negativity and boost your confidence. You will race better—I guarantee it.

TRAINING'S DONE

Ready to Race

At last, we're here. You've trained smart, fueled well, and prepared your mind for the task at hand. Now it's time to realize all the potential you've created. It's time to race.

"Racing" means different things to different people, but at the end of the day, we all have one goal in common: to do our very best. It's getting the best out of ourselves at the precise time and place we're targeting that's the tricky part. So this is where it's best to take tips from the pros.

Professional runners approach racing differently than most other runners. They spend significant time rehearsing the race in their minds and preparing mentally for everything they might encounter. They prepare strategies for dealing with the rough patches, and they adjust better during the race to get the most from the day—whatever that might be.

So, having worked with my fair share of pros, I'm going to offer you what I've seen work for them as well as the thousands of other runners I've coached. If you follow these steps, you will be well positioned to have the race of a lifetime . . . but even if you don't, you'll still get the best out of yourself on that day, which is all any of us can ask for.

Lesson #42: Race Recon

One thing that the pros always do is race reconnaissance, or "recon"—that is, they thoroughly research a course before they race on it. As you'll see in the ensuing chapters, they do this (and many other things) because they don't want any surprises on race day. The more they can prepare their brains for what's ahead, the less likely they'll be to have a pity party when they slow down on an uphill or lose time crossing a windy bridge. This holds true for every runner!

Thanks to the internet, GPS watches, and smartphones, investigating the course in advance doesn't have to be super time- or resource-intensive. In fact, most of the strategies I am about to suggest require nothing more than an internet connection and maybe 30 minutes out of your day.

Recon Strategy 1: Run the Course

The best recon is, if possible, to run most or all of the race course. If you live nearby or happen to visit the city in advance, take a day where you have easy miles and go experience the hills, flats, turns, straightaways, potholes, curbs, and other terrain features firsthand. Make note of any features that might affect your normal race strategy.

For example, there's a local trail race that starts with a flat half mile on the roads before turning into single track. I knew an athlete I had racing could get stuck if he was behind a pack as they hit the single track, so while he might have ordinarily gone out conservatively, we decided that he should run that first half mile hard enough to be in a good position before he and his competitors hit the single track.

If you can't run the full course in advance—and for destination races, many of us can't—I recommend using an easy day or prerace shakeout to run the last part of the course once you arrive at the race site. This will help you get a feel for how the end of the race will be when you are suffering the most. No surprises!

Recon Strategy 2: Study Course Maps

Most races now have course maps, including elevation charts, on their websites. Study the maps carefully and again, think about your strengths and weaknesses and your current fitness level to plan your best race strategy for the course. Plus, remember to think about how you want to think across the course.

One important note: Always make sure to look at the scale on elevation charts. Some races, particularly hilly ones, try to make their race course look flatter by changing the scale and extending the elevation chart. Make sure you look at the exact elevation change to determine just how steep the uphills and downhills are.

Recon Strategy 3: Research Results

One of the nice things about chip timing is that it's easy to look at past years' results online. Plus, for many races, you can even see intermediate splits for runners. Were there any sections that were markedly faster or slower than the average pace? If so, why? (Check against the course map for possible terrain challenges.) Once you study the course map, look for splits that match up to elevation changes. How much did runners slow down on the big hill?

If you know someone who has run your goal race, how did their time compare to their times on other courses, particularly courses you've run before? This information really helps you wrap your head around a goal finish time for the race, especially on challenging courses where you know you can't run your fastest time but want to run your best time for that course.

Recon Strategy 4: Look for GPS Data

If the race doesn't offer a course map or an elevation chart, you can usually do a quick online search, find someone who has run the course (on Strava or a similar site), and uploaded their GPS file. While chip timing offers some splits along the route, a runner's GPS watch data gives you every mile (or kilometer), and apps like Strava make finding this information easy. Seeing pace variations and trends in the data will be especially helpful on unfamiliar courses or courses with unique characteristics.

For instance, if you've never run the Boston Marathon before, you might want an idea of how much time you can expect to lose on Heartbreak Hill. If you see that runners who finish around your goal time lose 20 seconds per mile on that part of the course, you can go into the race feeling confident that even if you run slower on those uphill miles, you'll make it up elsewhere—probably on the next three downhill miles!

Recon Strategy 5: Read Race Reports

Lastly, online blogs, forums, and race reports are plentiful, as more and more runners share their race experiences. Some runners will even post GoPro or other video footage of their race on YouTube. Seek these sources out and mine them for details. The more firsthand information you can gain—especially visual information like photos and videos—the better prepared you will be to do two things.

One is visualize your race. We'll discuss this in the next lesson, but knowing as much as you can about the setting where you'll be running will help you mentally prepare for every potential race scenario.

The other thing to do with all of this information is to find a course that mimics what your race will be like and use it for your goal-pace workouts. If you can get on the race course itself, even better! If not, pick out the key characteristics of your course (pancake flat vs. rolling hills vs. steep inclines; pavement vs. track vs. dirt; sharp turns vs. long straightaways) and try to practice somewhere similar. This is the best way to prepare your body for what you'll demand of it on race day.

Lesson #43: Visualization

As mentioned, another important step in race preparation—whether for brand new runners or Olympians—is visualization. Once you have a sense of the course, you want to visualize the race dozens, even hundreds of times before you ever run the event.

Why? Because you want every element of the race to feel familiar.

Your brain hates surprises—that's when it panics and starts to shut your body down to protect you. However, your brain is also very plastic. Therefore, by repeatedly imagining how you want your race to go, your brain will become comfortable with the entire scenario. If you visualize it enough, the brain says "I've been here before, no problem" and gives your body permission to do what you've been training it to do.

You can practice visualizing almost anywhere. You can do it out on a run, in line at the grocery store, or sitting on the couch with your dog. The important thing is that you do it a lot.

The other important thing is that you don't just imagine things going perfectly. Yes, most of the time you want to visualize your ideal scenario. However, every once in a while, make sure you also visualize some contingency plans. Races don't always go exactly as planned! So figure out how you'll adapt if something less than ideal happens so you still can perform your best on the day.

For instance, what will you do if you're feeling more depleted than usual two thirds of the way through the race? What if you wind up in a gap where you expected to be surrounded by people, but you're alone? How will you deal with these things?

I had one athlete, Alice, who was planning to run a marathon with a pace group to achieve her goal time. She knew the pacer personally and knew that if she stuck with him, she'd get the time she wanted. Therefore, leading up to the race, she spent most of her time visualizing sticking to his back mile after mile, even if she felt tired, even if the pace pack thinned out. As race day approached, she realized she needed to consider another possible scenario: What if the pacer ran into problems and had to pull out? What would she do? She decided that if that happened, she would need to be able to change tactics and rely on her watch to get the pacing right. As a result, her brain was ready for the unexpected, and while it didn't happen—the pacer finished the race, pulling her to a personal best—she ran the race feeling confident that she would be ready for anything.

As this story illustrates, the goal is for your brain to be familiar with as many scenarios as possible, just in case they happen. If you can do this, nothing will rattle you on race day, and you'll be in the best position to get the most out of yourself.

Lesson #44: Pacing Plan

Like it or not, pacing is a huge part of racing. It can make or break your race. Start out too fast and you risk "hitting the wall" or "blowing up"—terms that sound unpleasant for good reason. Start out too slow and you might never be able to make up the time. It's a bit like Goldilocks and the three bears—when it comes to pacing, you want to run your race "juuuuuust right."

To get your pacing strategy right, you need to understand some basic concepts around pacing. There are three overarching pacing strategies:

- **Even splits**, or running the same pace for the entire race. If you are running a 3:00:00 marathon, your pace would be 1:30:00 for the first half and 1:30:00 for the second half.
- **Negative splits**, or running the first half of the race *slower* than the second half. This means that in the case of your 3:00:00 marathon, your time for the first half of the race would be slower than 1:30:00 (so, say, 1:31:30), and the second half of the race would be faster than 1:30:00 (so 1:28:30).

- **Positive splits**, or running the first half of the race *faster* than the second half. This is the inverse of negative splits, so for your 3:00:00 marathon you'd run 1:25:00 for the first half and then slow down to run 1:35:00 for the second half.

None of these strategies is inherently better or worse than the others; in fact, they all have their place in certain types of races and for certain types of runners.

For instance, in "short" races, lasting about 10 minutes or less, world record holders tend to run even or slightly positive splits. In longer races, they tend to run even or negative splits.

So while most of us aren't world record holders, if you're unsure which strategy to pick, you can't go wrong with even pacing. Keep in mind, of course, that even pacing doesn't mean even *effort*. The faster and farther you're running, the more effort and intensity those later miles are going to require to stay on pace. (Remember *Lesson #38: Go Zone to Race Your Best?*)

That said, in longer races, negative splitting can be advantageous. First, starting out slower than your target pace gives your body time to warm up. Second, it can help keep your brain happier longer so that by the end of the race, you feel like you're charging for the finish line instead of wondering how much longer you can survive. Finally, when you are able to pick up your pace in the second half of a race, you become the "passer" as opposed to the "passee." You're focused on finishing fast and picking off other runners one by one. What's a better confidence booster than that?

Once you've settled on your pacing strategy, it's a good idea to set some "benchmark" times to hit. For instance, if you're running a marathon and want to execute even splits, then it's a good idea to calculate what your time should be at 10K, half, and 20K so you know if you're on track. The purpose is to make things as simple as possible so you can focus on the task at hand (and for most of us, trying to add individual mile splits in our head is the opposite of simple).

Speaking of mile splits, it's not a bad thing to pay some attention to them; however, you do not want to rely on your watch's GPS calculations for this. Between lost signals, poor tangents (which we'll talk about shortly), and multiple other factors, your watch can get out of sync with the mile markers on the course. *But these mile markers are what matter.* The finish line is not going to move any closer just because your watch "says" you're already at mile 13.1 or 26.2. So if you're running with a GPS watch, turn off "auto-lap" and manually hit the "lap" button when you pass each mile marker. And if this isn't something you've done before, don't forget to add it to your prerace visualization!

Lesson #45: Mental Plan

Much like I encourage all of my athletes to have a race plan they'll follow, in terms of where they'll speed up, slow down, stay relaxed, or push hard, I also encourage them to have a mental plan. This is different from visualization, in that it involves creating an actual plan for the thoughts you want to have throughout the race.

How you want to construct your mental plan is up to you. Some athletes break down the race by distance: At mile 3, they want to think about X. At mile 6, they want to think about Y. Others will break it down by landmarks, such as the Queensborough Bridge in the New York City Marathon, or the Newton Hills in the Boston Marathon. However you choose to divvy up the race, make sure you do it intentionally and in a way you will remember.

To create a mental plan that adheres to the Go Zone method discussed in *Lesson #38: Go Zone to Race Your Best,* start by breaking your race into four parts: the start, the Fast Rhythm Zone, the Go Zone, and the Get-Time Zone. Then match your mental plan to your strategy for each part. For instance, if you are planning to run a half marathon and want to hold yourself back from going out too fast, you might choose to think "control" or "patience" at the start.

As you learned from the Go Zone, the most important part of the race to plan for is the second half. Later in the race, your mind can start to wander, and you can lose focus. It's also tempting to have a pity party if it's not going as well as you want. In these instances, you need a way to get your brain back in the game to get the most out of yourself so you can finish feeling satisfied that you did all that you could.

Therefore, construct your mental plan by asking not only

"How do I want to think?"

but also

"What strategies can I use to pull myself back if I stray from my mental plan?"

Finally, write it all down! By committing your plan to paper, you can review it over and over until it becomes second nature.

If this is all feeling a bit abstract, let me offer a real example from my own running:

When I won the National Championship in the trail marathon, I developed a specific thinking strategy for the race. This was especially important since the course was very different from a regular road marathon course. The start included 8 miles of uphill climbing to over 5,000 feet of elevation. Then, the course rolled along undulating terrain until mile 20, where it took a sudden steep and very technical last 10K to the finish line.

In a normal marathon, I try to run a slightly negative split, as I'm trying to save my mental and physical energy for the last 10K. Due to the race course, saving my energy to expend it at the end wouldn't work in the Championship race. I knew I'd need to exert more energy (mentally and physically) in the first 8 miles due to the climb. I had to wrap my head around this, since it was different than my normal mindset in the marathon. My mental plan was to think "Strong but efficient" as I climbed the first 8 miles. This allowed my mind to get comfortable with exerting more effort while also trying to do it as economically as possible.

Once the climb was over, my mind switched to "cruise and float." Over the next 12 miles, I wanted to relax as much as possible at race pace. I knew I would be more tired than usual due to the climb, but if I had the right mindset, I could simply focus on covering ground. This is also when I executed what I think is one of the most powerful mental strategies, "smile through the suffering." As mentioned, the brain can be manipulated, and smiling is a great way to trick it to think things are not as bad as they are. Whenever I got tired, I would smile. (And I smiled a lot!)

I knew the last 10K was all downhill, so I didn't worry about being a little more tired than I'd like at 20 miles in a marathon. But that didn't mean I could forgo a good thinking plan. If you've run a marathon, you know how sore your legs are in the last 10K. For me, I was about to absolutely trash my legs with the steep, technical downhill running at sub-6-minute pace, so I knew I'd better have my mind right. For this section, where I knew every step would be painful, I simply thought "I don't have to run tomorrow. Lean into it." This helped me fly down the hills and better tolerate the pain in my quads.

The result was one of my best-run marathons and a National Championship win.

Lesson #46: Let Go/Latch On

A common mistake runners make is going too hard too early in the race. There are plenty of reasons for this, from the adrenaline surge when the gun goes off to "I just felt good." Many of these can be mitigated by experience, but one reason that comes up with my veteran runners over and over again is seeing the competition take off. They're there to race, so they don't want to let their competitors run away!

This competitive spirit is wonderful—it's what makes racing fun. However, if you let it get the best of you early in a race, you'll oftentimes pay for it later. To help runners avoid this mistake, I've come up with the following saying:

"Let go early. Latch on later."

Early in a race, it's important that you run *your* race. If somebody else wants to go faster, let them go. Typically, the people who go out too fast will come back to you later, or they might be in better shape. Let them go and focus on executing your pace plan and mental plan.

Once you pass halfway, however, the strategy changes. Now, if someone passes you, you have to latch on. Move right behind them and make it your only goal to stick to their back. Think of them as your "tow to the finish line." If you can just stay with them, you'll arrive at the finish line before you know it . . . and maybe even have the chance to out-sprint them!

I used this strategy during my fastest marathon. In the first half of the race, I stayed controlled, but as I began to fatigue, a runner passed me. Instead of feeling defeated, I said, "This is great. He's my ride." I latched onto him, and it re-energized my race. I was able to finish strong, despite fatigue, because I took that split-second opportunity to latch on.

So, to sum up this lesson: In the first half of the race, run your own race; **let** faster people go. In the second half, when you want to be more competitive and it's easy to slow down, **latch on.** Let your competitors tow you to the finish line.

Lesson #47: Taking Tangents

When a course is measured, it's measured on the shortest route possible. This means that to get from the start to the finish of a 5K, 10K, half-, or full marathon, you don't want to follow the center of the road the whole time, because you'll actually run farther! Instead you want to run the way they measure the course: taking "tangents," i.e., the most direct route possible.

To do this, always look up ahead for what's coming. Especially in large races where you're stuck in a "herd," you want to stay alert to any turns or curves up ahead so you can get in the best position to run the tangent. Over many miles, these small adjustments can make a huge difference.

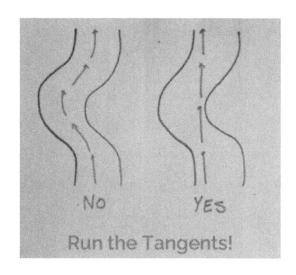

No   Yes

Run the Tangents!

Finally, as with every other race tactic, taking the tangents is something you need to practice! Particularly if you'll be facing a windy course or one with a lot of turns, you want to practice on routes with these features—ideally during one of your goal-pace workouts. And if you can get some running friends to come along, all the better. Have them run close to you, and practice jockeying within the pack to run the shortest tangent. You'll find that it can take some patience and a bit of assertiveness, but that's what practice is for!

Lesson #48: Gain Ground with Corners & Hills

There are two key places in a race where runners instinctively tend to slow down: when approaching corners (taking those tangents we talked about!) and cresting the tops of hills. However, if you can pick up the pace in these two key spots, you can gain time and put distance between yourself and your competitors.

First up: corners. It feels natural to slow down as you approach a corner, especially in the second half of a race when you're getting tired. This makes it even more important to do the opposite:

Pick up the pace. Focus on a faster rhythm.

Athletes lose so much momentum on corners, but this is a big mistake. It's difficult, when tired, to get your cadence going again after you slow down. So attack the corners! Think "quick feet, quick corner." By doing this, you can avoid breaking your momentum and keep it going all the way to the finish. Plus, if you're neck-and-neck with a competitor, quick corners might be where you can beat them!

Next: hills. Most runners run to the top of a hill and then slow down before continuing the race. My high school cross country coach, Coach Pruitt, gave great advice to counter this tendency: "You don't just run to the top of hills, you run *over* hills."

What you want to do is continue pushing at the top of the hill just as hard as you were pushing to get to the top. If you can use those 5–10 seconds after you reach the top of the hill to reestablish a faster pace (running "over" the hill), you will quickly regain a faster cadence. Then, if you have a downhill coming next, that quicker turnover will help you take advantage of gravity and make up some of the time you lost going up. Don't miss out on free speed!

Lesson #49: Effort on the Day

Despite even the best preparation, not every race goes exactly as planned. There can be wind, humidity, or rain, or maybe you just don't feel great. The question is: Can you still get the most out of yourself?

Part of being a great racer is the ability to get the most out of yourself on race day, no matter what. To never give up on yourself. To pull your mind back from a pity party or defeatist mindset so you can still perform your best on the day.

Meb Keflezighi, Desi Linden, and Deena Kastor are all excellent examples of this type of racer. If you look across their careers, they always seem to get the most out of themselves in every race, even if it doesn't go exactly as planned. (For them, the plan is usually to win the race. And we know they didn't win every single one!) Even when they're a little off on the day, they only miss the mark by a little bit; the race is rarely a catastrophe. Comparatively some other athletes can perform amazingly if they're "on" and feeling great, but if things don't quite go exactly as planned, they fall apart and have really poor races.

In other words, runners like Meb, Desi, and Deena consistently race well. They don't always achieve their goals, but they don't have many stinker races, either.

We want to be like them. Our goal at every race should be to leverage all of our race skills: our pacing plan, our visualization, and our mental plan. We need to train ourselves to think: "I can go out and have a successful race no matter the conditions. No matter how I feel, no matter the competition, I will finish knowing I did my best on that day."

Maybe your time won't be exactly what you wanted, and maybe you won't place as high in the results as you thought you could. However, if you strive to get the best out of yourself at every race, you can finish feeling satisfied that you did your best. And more than that: Giving your all at every race gives you the best possible chance of having that stellar race outcome. It's truly a win-win.

Lesson #50: The Post-Race Eval

You've crossed the finish line. The race is done. Congratulations! No matter how it went, you put a ton of time, effort, and energy into preparing for it, and that's something to be proud of. But you're not done yet. After settling down from the race, it's time to look at exactly what all of that preparation added up to. It's time to evaluate your race.

When looking at a really good or really bad race, it's easy to get emotional, so I find it best to start as objectively as possible. That means starting with numbers: your race splits. How do those match up against the plan you had going into the race? If you intended to negative split, did you do that? Was the first part of your race too fast, too slow, or right on target? These are the questions you want to ask by looking purely at the numbers.

Next, it's time to critique your performance more subjectively. If you were to run the same race again, what would you do differently? Maybe you were on pace through halfway but then lost focus, lost your pace group, and couldn't get started again.

302

If you could do it over, you might concentrate on staying focused and sticking with your pace group no matter what.

On the flip side, what did you do well? Maybe you dialed in your nutrition perfectly. Maybe you kept your effort up, even though your splits don't reflect it. Whatever went well, make sure you verbalize it, aloud or in writing, so that you can remember to do it again.

Finally, think through the mental side of the race. Did you execute your mental race plan the way you had hoped? If so, what preparation helped you? If not, what could you work on to improve for next time? It's important to be as honest as you can about the mental side of racing, because this is the only way to determine if what kept you from achieving your goal—or helped you achieve it!—was mental or physical.

The whole point of this exercise is to figure out what to adjust for your next race. So as difficult as it can be, embrace the failures—they give you the most information about what you can improve. Most times, it's the training (mental or physical) that you'll wind up adjusting. If you keep getting dropped by the competition on hills, then you need to find a way to do more hill training. If you keep going to a negative place mentally late in the race, then it's time to find some mental strategies to practice on your long runs.

Sometimes, however, it's the race strategy itself that needs to be adjusted. Olympian Lorraine Moller used to race another runner from Australia regularly. In every race, at some point late in the race, the Australian woman would take off her arm sleeves and then sprint all the way to the finish. When she did this, Lorraine could never catch her. So Lorraine revised her race plan: At the next race, as soon as Lorraine saw the woman starting to peel down one arm sleeve, Lorraine took off. The woman was so rattled, she never even got the arm sleeves off! And more importantly, Lorraine beat her.

You may not be an Olympian like Lorraine, but this is a great example of taking information from disappointing races and using it to improve the next one. Post-race evaluations are just one more part of the process! Everyone makes mistakes, from the pros on down, and everyone wants to do better. So embrace the process, and look forward to doing better. I know you can.

McMillan Training Plans

The pages that follow contain sample training plans. The plans are arranged by goal distance as well as by the number of days you run per week (e.g., 10K plan with 4–5 days running per week).

Start by finding the plans that match—or come close to matching—the distance of your peak race. I've named them 5K, 10K, half-marathon, and marathon, but if, for example, you are training for a 10-mile race, you can easily use the half-marathon plan.

Next, think about the number of days per week you can run. This goes back to the first lessons of running training that we covered: Be honest about the training you can commit to completing consistently! If you're unsure, choose the "easier" plan. Most of us will be tempted to do a little bit more than what was written, and that always feels much better than falling short of completing a plan that was too ambitious.

Finally, please understand that these are not surefire recipes for success. In fact, I wrote a whole other book about how to tweak training plans like these so you can get the most out of your own unique strengths and weaknesses. For a deeper dive into that methodology, check out *You (Only Faster): Training Plans to Help You Train Smarter and Run Faster.*

MCMILLAN RUNNING

McMillan **5K** Training Plan: **2-3 DAYS** of running per week

WEEK	PHASE	1	2	3	4	5	6	7
1	Mileage Base	OFF or XT	30-40 min	OFF or XT	40-50 min	OFF	OFF or XT	LR: 60-70 min
2	Prep - Hills	OFF or XT	30-40 min	OFF or XT	Hills: 6-8 reps	OFF	OFF or XT	LR: 60-70 min
3	Prep - Stamina	OFF or XT	40-50 min	OFF or XT	PR: 40-50 min w/ last 15-25 min fast	OFF	OFF or XT	LR: 60-70 min
4	Prep - Hills	OFF or XT	40-50 min	OFF or XT	Hills: 8-10 reps	OFF	OFF or XT	40-50 min
5	Prep - Stamina	OFF or XT	40-50 min	OFF or XT	PR: 40-50 min w/ last 20-30 min fast	OFF	OFF or XT	LR: 70-80 min
6	Prep - Hills	OFF or XT	50-60 min	OFF or XT	Hills: 10-12 reps	OFF	OFF or XT	LR: 70-80 min
7	5K	OFF or XT	50-60 min	OFF or XT	FR: 3 x 6 min w/ 3 min jog	OFF	OFF or XT	PR: 60-70 min w/ last 20-30 min fast
8	5K	OFF or XT	40-50 min	OFF or XT	FR: 10-12 x 1 min w/ 2 min jog	OFF	OFF or XT	LR: 70-80 min
9	5K	OFF or XT	50-60 min	OFF or XT	FR: 8-10 x 2 min w/ 3 min jog	OFF	OFF or XT	PR: 60-70 min w/ last 20-30 min fast
10	5K	OFF or XT	40-50 min	OFF or XT	FR: 3 x 6 min w/ 3 min jog	OFF	OFF or XT	PR: 70-80 w/ last 10-20 min fast
11	Peak	OFF or XT	40-50 min	OFF or XT	FR: 6-8 x 2 min w/ 3 min jog	OFF	OFF or XT	45 min
12	Peak	OFF or XT	30-40 min	OFF or XT	FR: 8-10 x 1 min w/ 2 min jog	OFF	OFF or XT	RACE: 5K

KEY: min = minutes
km = kilometers
Hills = Hill Workout (p. 217)
PR = Progression Run (p. 220)

Mi = miles
OFF = No exercise
LR = Long Run (p. 100)

m = meters
XT = cross-training
FR = Fartlek Run (p. 131)

MCMILLAN RUNNING

McMillan **5K** Training Plan: **4-5 DAYS** of running per week

WEEK	PHASE	1	2	3	4	5	6	7
1	Prep - Hills	OFF	40-50 min	OFF, XT or 40-60 min	Hills: 6-8 reps	OFF, XT or 40-60 min	50-60 min	LR: 80-90 min
2	Prep - Stamina	OFF	LS: 10 x 20 sec w/ 1 min jog	OFF, XT or 40-60 min	TI: 3-4 x 2000m w/ 400m jog	OFF, XT or 40-60 min	50-60 min	LR: 90-105 min
3	Prep - Hills	OFF	80-90 min	OFF, XT or 40-60 min	Hills: 8-10 reps	OFF, XT or 40-60 min	50-60 min	LR: 90-105 min
4	Prep - Stamina	OFF	LS: 15 x 20 sec w/ 1 min jog	OFF, XT or 40-60 min	TR: 2-4 miles	OFF, XT or 40-60 min	50-60 min	LR: 75-90 min
5	Prep - Hills	OFF	80-90 min	OFF, XT or 40-60 min	Hills: 10-12 reps	OFF, XT or 40-60 min	50-60 min	FFLR: 90 w/ last 10-20 min fast
6	Prep - Stamina	OFF	LS: 20 x 20 sec w/ 1 min jog	OFF, XT or 40-60 min	CI: 8-10 x 1000m w/ 200m jog	OFF, XT or 40-60 min	50-60 min	LR: 90-105 min
7	5K	OFF	50-60 min	OFF, XT or 40-60 min	SP: 4 x 1 mile w/ 800m jog	OFF, XT or 40-60 min	50-60 min	FFLR: 90 w/ last 10-20 min fast
8	5K	OFF	80-90 min	OFF, XT or 40-60 min	SP: 16-20 x 200m w/ 200m jog	OFF, XT or 40-60 min	50-60 min	50-60 min
9	5K	OFF	TR: 2-4 miles	OFF, XT or 40-60 min	SP: 10-12 x 400m w/ 200m jog	OFF, XT or 40-60 min	50-60 min	FFLR: 90 w/ last 10-20 min fast
10	5K	OFF	LS: 8 x 30 sec w/ 1 min jog	OFF, XT or 40-60 min	SP: 6 x 800m w/ 400m jog	OFF, XT or 40-60 min	50-60 min	LR: 90-105 min
11	Peak	OFF	50-60 min	OFF, XT or 40-50 min	TR: 2-4 miles	OFF, XT or 40-50 min	40-50 min	PR: 60 min w/ last 10 min fast
12	Peak	OFF	SP: 8-10 x 400m w/ 200m jog	OFF, XT or 30-40 min	FR: 6-8 x 1 min w/ 1 min jog	OFF, XT or 40-50 min	30-40 min	RACE: 5K

KEY: min = minutes
km = kilometers
SP = Speed Workout (p. 129)
FR = Fartlek Run (p. 131)
PR = Progression Run (p. 220)
FFLR = Fast Finish Long Run (p. 211)

Mi = miles
OFF = No exercise
Hills = Hill Workout (p. 217)
CI = Cruise Intervals (p. 117)
TR = Tempo Run (p. 114)

m = meters
XT = cross-training
LR = Long Run (p. 100)
TI = Tempo Intervals (p. 115)
LS = Leg Speed (p. 142)

© Greg McMillan, McMillan Running LLC, 2021 All Rights Reserved, www.mcmillanrunning.com

310

McMillan **5K** Training Plan: **6-7 DAYS** of running per week

WEEK	PHASE	1	2	3	4	5	6	7
1	Prep - Hills	OFF, XT or 40-60 min	70-80 min	50-60 min	Hills: 8-10 reps	OFF, XT or 40-60 min	60-70 min	LR: 90-105 min
2	Prep - Stamina	OFF, XT or 40-60 min	LS: 10 x 20 sec w/ 1 min jog	50-60 min	TI: 4-5 x 2000m w/ 400m jog	OFF, XT or 40-60 min	60-70 min	LR: 90-105 min
3	Prep - Hills	OFF, XT or 40-60 min	80-90 min	50-60 min	Hills: 10-12 reps	OFF, XT or 40-60 min	60-70 min	LR: 105-120 min
4	Prep - Stamina	OFF, XT or 40-60 min	LS: 15 x 20 sec w/ 1 min jog	50-60 min	TR: 2-4 miles	OFF, XT or 40-60 min	60-70 min	LR: 80-90 min
5	Prep - Hills	OFF, XT or 40-60 min	80-90 min	50-60 min	Hills: 10-12 reps	OFF, XT or 40-60 min	60-70 min	LR: 105-120 min
6	Prep - Stamina	OFF, XT or 40-60 min	LS: 20 x 20 sec w/ 1 min jog	50-60 min	CI: 10-12 x 1000m w/ 200m jog	OFF, XT or 40-60 min	60-70 min	LR: 90-105 min
7	5K	OFF, XT or 40-60 min	TR: 3-5 miles	50-60 min	SP: 5-6 x 1 mile w/ 800m jog + 4 x 200m w/ 200m jog	OFF, XT or 40-60 min	60-70 min	FFLR: 90-105 min w/ last 10 min fast
8	5K	OFF, XT or 40-60 min	PR: 60-70 min w/ last 5 min fast	50-60 min	SP: 20-24 x 200m w/ 200m jog	OFF, XT or 40-60 min	60-70 min	LR: 90-105 min
9	5K	OFF, XT or 40-60 min	TR: 3-5 miles	50-60 min	SP: 8-10 x 300m w/ 400m jog	OFF, XT or 40-60 min	60-70 min	FFLR: 90-105 min w/ last 10 min fast
10	5K	OFF, XT or 40-60 min	PR: 60-70 min w/ last 5 min fast	50-60 min	SP: 12-16 x 400m w/ 200m jog	OFF, XT or 40-60 min	60-70 min	LR: 90-105 min
11	Peak	OFF or 40-50 min	LS: 15 x 20 sec w/ 1 min jog	40-50 min	TR: 2-4 miles	OFF or 40-50 min	40-50 min	PR: 70-80 min w/ last 10 min fast
12	Peak	OFF or 30-40 min	CI: 4-5 x 1000m w/ 200m jog	30-40 min	FR: 8-10 x 1 min w/ 1 min jog	OFF or 30-40 min	30-40 min	RACE: 5K

KEY: min = minutes
km = kilometers
SP = Speed Workout (p. 129)
FR = Fartlek Run (p. 131)
PR = Progression Run (p. 220)
FFLR = Fast Finish Long Run (p. 211)

Mi = miles
OFF = No exercise
Hills = Hill Workout (p. 217)
CI = Cruise Intervals (p. 117)
TR = Tempo Run (p. 114)

m = meters
XT = cross-training
LR = Long Run (p. 100)
TI = Tempo Intervals (p. 115)
LS = Leg Speed (p. 142)

MCMILLAN RUNNING

McMillan **10K** Training Plan: **2-3 DAYS** of running per week

WEEK	PHASE	1	2	3	4	5	6	7
1	Mileage Base	OFF or XT	40-50 min	OFF or XT	40-50 min	OFF	OFF or XT	LR: 70-80 min
2	Prep - Stamina	OFF or XT	40-50 min	OFF or XT	PR: 40-50 min w/ last 15-25 min fast	OFF	OFF or XT	LR: 80-90 min
3	Prep - Hills	OFF or XT	50-60 min	OFF or XT	Hills: 6-8 reps	OFF	OFF or XT	LR: 90-105 min
4	Prep - Stamina	OFF or XT	30-40 min	OFF or XT	PR: 40-50 min w/ last 20-30 min fast	OFF	OFF or XT	LR: 90-105 min
5	Prep - Hills	OFF or XT	50-60 min	OFF or XT	Hills: 8-10 reps	OFF	OFF or XT	LR: 90-105 min
6	10K	OFF or XT	50-60 min	OFF or XT	FR: 4-5 x 2 min on 1 min off	OFF	OFF or XT	LR: 90-105 min
7	10K	OFF or XT	50-60 min	OFF or XT	FR: 10-12 x 1 min on 1 min off	OFF	OFF or XT	PR: 60-70 min w/ last 20 min fast
8	10K	OFF or XT	50-60 min	OFF or XT	TR: 2-3 mi	OFF	OFF or XT	LR: 90-105 min
9	10K	OFF or XT	40-50 min	OFF or XT	FR: 15-20 x 1 min on 1 min off	OFF	OFF or XT	PR: 60-70 min w/ last 20 min fast
10	10K	OFF or XT	40-50 min	OFF or XT	FR: 4-5 x 3 min on 2 min off	OFF	OFF or XT	LR: 80-90 min
11	Peak	OFF or XT	40-50 min	OFF or XT	FR: 20-25 x 1 min on 1 min off	OFF	OFF or XT	PR: 60-70 min w/ last 20 min fast
12	Peak	OFF or XT	30-40 min	OFF or XT	FR: 4-5 x 1 min w/ 1 min	OFF	OFF	RACE: 10K

KEY: min = minutes   Mi = miles   m = meters
km = kilometers   OFF = No exercise   XT = cross-training
Hills = Hill Workout (p. 217)   LR = Long Run (p. 100)   FR = Fartlek Run (p. 131)
PR = Progression Run (p. 220)   TR = Tempo Run (p. 114)

312

MCMILLAN RUNNING

McMillan **10K** Training Plan: **4-5 DAYS** of running per week

WEEK	PHASE	1	2	3	4	5	6	7
1	Prep - Hills	OFF	50-60 min	OFF or 40-60 min	Hills: 8-10 reps	OFF or 40-60 min	50-60 min	LR: 80-100 min
2	Prep - Stamina	OFF	TR: 2-4 miles	OFF or 40-60 min	TI: 3-4 x 2000m w/ 400m jog	OFF or 40-60 min	50-60 min	LR: 90-105 min
3	Prep - Hills	OFF	LS: 10 x 30 sec w/ 1 min jog	OFF or 40-60 min	Hills: 10-12 reps	OFF or 40-60 min	50-60 min	LR: 90-105 min
4	Prep - Stamina	OFF	70-80 min	OFF or 40-60 min	TI: 6 x 1 mile w/ 800m jog	OFF or 40-60 min	50-60 min	LR: 80-90 min
5	Prep - Stamina	OFF	70-80 min	OFF or 40-60 min	CI: 6-8 x 800 w/ 200m jog + 4 x 100m w/ 100m	OFF or 40-60 min	50-60 min	LR: 105-120 min
6	10K	OFF	TR: 3-5 miles	OFF or 40-60 min	SP: 12-14 x 400m w/ 200m jog + 4 x 200m w/ 200m jog	OFF or 40-60 min	50-60 min	LR: 105-120 min
7	10K	OFF	50-60 min	OFF or 40-60 min	TI: 2 miles, jog 5 min, 4 x 1 mile w/ 3-4 min jog	OFF or 40-60 min	50-60 min	LR: 90-105 min
8	10K	OFF	TR: 3-5 miles	OFF or 40-60 min	SP: 20-24 x 200m w/ 200m jog	OFF or 40-60 min	50-60 min	LR: 80-90 min
9	10K	OFF	PR: 50-60 min w/ last 15 min fast	OFF or 40-60 min	TI: 2 x 2 miles w/ 5 min jog + 2 x 1 mile w/ 3 min jog	OFF or 40-60 min	50-60 min	LR: 90-105 min
10	10K	OFF	LS: 10 x 30 sec w/ 1 min jog	OFF or 40-60 min	SP: 4-5 x 1 mile w/ 800m jog	OFF or 40-60 min	50-60 min	FFLR: 90 min w/ last 10-20 min fast
11	Peak	OFF	FR: 5 x 2 min w/ 1 min jog	OFF or 40-50 min	TI: 3 x 2 miles w/ 5 min jog	OFF or 40-50 min	40-50 min	PR: 70-80 w/ last 10 min fast
12	Peak	OFF	SP: 8-10 x 400m w/ 200m jog	OFF or 30-40 min	FR: 5-6 x 1 min w/ 1 min jog	OFF or 30-40 min	30-40 min	RACE: 10K

KEY: min = minutes
km = kilometers
SP = Speed Workout (p. 129)
FR = Fartlek Run (p. 131)
PR = Progression Run (p. 220)
FFLR = Fast Finish Long Run (p. 211)

Mi = miles
OFF = No exercise
Hills = Hill Workout (p. 217)
CI = Cruise Intervals (p. 117)
TR = Tempo Run (p. 114)

m = meters
XT = cross-training
LR = Long Run (p. 100)
TI = Tempo Intervals (p. 115)
LS = Leg Speed (p. 142)

MCMILLAN RUNNING

McMillan **10K** Training Plan: **6-7 DAYS** of running per week

WEEK	PHASE	1	2	3	4	5	6	7
1	Prep - Hills	OFF or 40-60 min	LS: 10-12 x 30 sec w/ 1 min jog	50-60 min	Hills: 8-10 reps	OFF or 40-60 min	60-70 min	LR: 90-105 min
2	Prep - Hills	OFF or 40-60 min	TR: 2-4 miles	50-60 min	Hills: 10-12 reps	OFF or 40-60 min	60-70 min	LR: 90-105 min
3	Prep - Stamina	OFF or 40-60 min	LS: 10-12 x 30 sec w/ 1 min jog	50-60 min	TI: 6 x 1 mile w/ 400m jog	OFF or 40-60 min	60-70 min	LR: 105-120 min
4	Prep - Hills	OFF or 40-60 min	PR: 60-70 min w/ last 10 min fast	50-60 min	Hills: 10-12 reps	OFF or 40-60 min	60-70 min	LLR: 90 min
5	Prep - Stamina	OFF or 40-60 min	TR: 3-5 miles	50-60 min	CI: 6-8 x 800 w/ 200m jog + 4 x 100m w/ 100m jog	OFF or 40-60 min	60-70 min	LR: 105-120 min
6	10K	OFF or 40-60 min	PR: 60-70 min w/ last 10 min fast	50-60 min	SP: 12-16 x 400m w/ 200m jog	OFF or 40-60 min	60-70 min	LR: 105-120 min
7	10K	OFF or 40-60 min	SP: 8 x 200m w/ 200m jog	50-60 min	TI: 2 miles, jog 5 mn then 4 x 1 mile w/ 3-4 min jog	OFF or 40-60 min	60-70 min	FFLR: 90-105 min w/ last 10-20 min fast
8	10K	OFF or 40-60 min	TR: 3-5 miles	50-60 min	SP: 20-24 x 200m w/ 200m jog	OFF or 40-60 min	60-70 min	LLR: 90 min
9	10K	OFF or 40-60 min	SP: 6 x 400m w/ 200m jog	50-60 min	TI: 2 x 2 miles w/ 5 min jog then 2 x 1 mile w/ 3 min jog	OFF or 40-60 min	60-70 min	LR: 105-120 min
10	10K	OFF or 40-60 min	TR: 3-5 miles	50-60 min	SP: 12-16 x 400m w/ 200m jog	OFF or 40-60 min	60-70 min	LR: 90-105 min
11	Peak	OFF or 40-50 min	LS: 10-12 x 30 sec w/ 1 min jog	40-50 min	TI: 3 x 2 miles w/ 5 min jog	OFF or 40-50 min	40-50 min	PR: 70-80 min w/ last 10 min fast
12	Peak	OFF or 30-40 min	SP: 8-10 x 400m w/ 200m jog	30-40 min	FR: 8-10 x 1 min w/ 1 min jog	OFF or 30-40 min	30-40 min	RACE: 10K

KEY: min = minutes
km = kilometers
SP = Speed Workout (p. 129)
FR = Fartlek Run (p. 131)
PR = Progression Run (p. 220)
FFLR = Fast Finish Long Run (p. 211)

Mi = miles
OFF = No exercise
Hills = Hill Workout (p. 217)
CI = Cruise Intervals (p. 117)
TR = Tempo Run (p. 114)

m = meters
XT = cross-training
LR = Long Run (p. 100)
TI = Tempo Intervals (p. 115)
LS = Leg Speed (p. 142)

314

MCMILLAN
RUNNING

McMillan **HALF MARATHON** Training Plan: **2-3 DAYS** of running per week

WEEK	PHASE	1	2	3	4	5	6	7
1	Mileage Base	OFF	30-45 min	XT or 30-45 min	30-45 min	OFF or XT	XT or 30-45 min	LR: 45-60 min
2	Mileage Base	OFF	30-45 min	XT or 30-45 min	30-45 min	OFF or XT	XT or 30-45 min	LR: 70-80 min
3	Mileage Base	OFF	45-60 min	XT or 30-45 min	45-60 min	OFF or XT	XT or 30-45 min	LR: 45-60 min
4	Mileage Base	OFF	45-60 min	XT or 30-45 min	45-60 min	OFF or XT	XT or 30-45 min	LR: 80-90 min
5	Half Marathon	OFF	45-60 min	XT or 30-45 min	PR: 50-60 min w/ last 15 min fast	OFF or XT	XT or 30-45 min	LR: 60-75 min
6	Half Marathon	OFF	70-80 min	XT or 30-45 min	CI: 4 x 800m w/ 200m jog	OFF or XT	XT or 30-45 min	LR: 90-105 min
7	Half Marathon	OFF	70-80 min	XT or 30-45 min	TI: 2 x 1 miles w/ 5 min jog	OFF or XT	XT or 30-45 min	LR: 105-120 min
8	Half Marathon	OFF	80-100 min	XT or 30-45 min	FR: 10-15 x 1 min w/ 1 min jog	OFF or XT	XT or 30-45 min	LR: 90-105 min
9	Half Marathon	OFF	45-60 min	XT or 30-45 min	TI: 2 x 2 miles w/ 5 min jog	OFF or XT	XT or 30-45 min	FFLR: 105-120 min w/ last 20-30 min fast
10	Half Marathon	OFF	80-100 min	XT or 30-45 min	FR: 10-15 x 1 min w/ 1 min jog	OFF or XT	XT or 30-45 min	FFLR: 105-120 min w/ last 20-30 min fast
11	Peak	OFF	40 min	XT or 30-45 min	TI: 3 x 2 miles w/ 5 min jog	OFF or XT	XT or 30 min	LR: 8-10 miles
12	Peak	OFF	40 min	XT or 30-45 min	FR: 5-6 x 1 min w/ 1 min jog	OFF or XT	XT or 20 min	RACE: Half Marathon

KEY: min = minutes   Mi = miles   m = meters
km = kilometers   OFF = No exercise   XT = cross-training
LR = Long Run (p. 100)   FR = Fartlek Run (p. 131)   CI = Cruise Intervals (p. 117)
PR = Progression Run (p. 220)   TI = Tempo Intervals (p. 115)   FFLR = Fast Finish Long Run (p. 211)

MCMILLAN RUNNING

McMillan **HALF MARATHON** Training Plan: **4-5 DAYS** of running per week

WEEK	PHASE	1	2	3	4	5	6	7
1	Prep - Hills	OFF	40-50 min	XT or 40-60 min	Hills: 6-8 reps	OFF or 40-60 mi	50-60 min	LR: 90-105 min
2	Mileage Base	OFF	50-60 min	XT or 40-60 min	80-90 min	OFF or 40-60 mi	50-60 min	LR: 90-105 min
3	Prep - Hills	OFF	FR: 8-10 x 1 min on 1 min off	XT or 40-60 min	Hills: 8-10 reps	OFF or 40-60 mi	50-60 min	LR: 105-120 min
4	Half Marathon	OFF	50-60 min	XT or 40-60 min	CI: 8-10 x 1000m w/ 200m jog	OFF or 40-60 mi	50-60 min	LR: 105-120 min
5	Half Marathon	OFF	80-90 min	XT or 40-60 min	TI: 4-5 x 2000m w/ 400m jog	OFF or 40-60 mi	50-60 min	LR: 14-18 miles
6	Half Marathon	OFF	LS: 50-60 min w/ 10 x 15 sec fast w/ 1 min easy within run	XT or 40-60 min	TR: 3-5 miles	OFF or 40-60 mi	50-60 min	LR: 14-18 miles
7	Half Marathon	OFF	80-90 min	XT or 40-60 min	SP: 6-8 x 1200m w/600m jog	OFF or 40-60 mi	50-60 min	FFLR: 14-16 miles w/ last 2-4 miles fast
8	Half Marathon	OFF	PR: 50-60 w/ last 10 min fast	XT or 40-60 min	TI: 3 x 2 miiles w/ 5min jog	OFF or 40-60 mi	50-60 min	LR: 14-18 miles
9	Half Marathon	OFF	80-90 min	XT or 40-60 min	TR: 5-7 miles	OFF or 40-60 mi	50-60 min	FFLR: 14-16 miles w/ last 2-4 miles fast
10	Half Marathon	OFF	LS: 50-60 min w/ 10 x 15 sec fast w/ 1 min easy within run	XT or 40-60 min	SP: 5-6 x 1 mile w/ 800m jog	OFF or 40-60 mi	50-60 min	LR: 105-120 min
11	Peak	OFF	FR: 8-10 x 1 min on 1 min off	XT or 40-50 min	SS: 6-8 miles	OFF or 40-50 min	40-50 min	FFLR: 12-14 miles w/ last 2-4 miles @ goal HM pace
12	Peak	OFF	CI: 4-5 x 1000m w/ 200m jog	XT or 30-40 min	FR: 8-10 x 1 min w/ 1 min jog	OFF or 30-40 min	30-40 min	RACE: Half Marathon

KEY: min = minutes
km = kilometers
LR = Long Run (p. 100)
PR = Progression Run (p. 220)
SP = Speed Workout (p. 129)
LS = Leg Speed (p. 142)

MI = miles
OFF = No exercise
FR = Fartlek Run (p. 131)
TI = Tempo Intervals (p. 115)
SS = Steady State Run (p. 112)
Hills = Hill Workout (p. 217)

m = meters
XT = cross-training
CI = Cruise Intervals (p. 117)
FFLR = Fast Finish Long Run (p. 211)
TR = Tempo Run (p. 114)

MCMILLAN RUNNING

McMillan **HALF MARATHON** Training Plan: **6-7 DAYS** of running per week

WEEK	PHASE	1	2	3	4	5	6	7
1	Prep - Speed + Hills	XT or 55-65 min	FR: 6-7 x 2 min w/ 1 min jog	60-70 min	Hills: 6-8 reps	XT or 55-65 min	60-70 min	LR: 105-120 min
2	Prep - Speed + Hills	XT or 55-65 min	FR: 5-6 x 3 min w/ 2 min jog	60-70 min	Hills: 8-10 reps	XT or 55-65 min	60-70 min	LR: 105-120 min
3	Prep - Speed + Hills	XT or 55-65 min	FR: 10-12 x 1 min w/ 1 min jog	60-70 min	Hills: 10-12 reps	XT or 55-65 min	60-70 min	LR: 105-120 min
4	Half Marathon	XT or 55-65 min	60-70 min	60-70 min	CI: 8-10 x 1000m w/ 200m jog	XT or 55-65 min	60-70 min	LR: 105-120 min
5	Half Marathon	XT or 55-65 min	PR: 80-90 min w/ last 20 minutes fast	60-70 min	SP: 5-7 x 1 mile w/ 800m jog	XT or 55-65 min	60-70 min	LR: 105-120 min
6	Half Marathon	XT or 55-65 min	60-70 min	60-70 min	TR: 3-5 miles	XT or 55-65 min	60-70 min	LR: 14-18 miles
7	Half Marathon	XT or 55-65 min	PR: 80-90 min w/ last 20 minutes fast	60-70 min	SP: 6-8 x 1200m w/ 600m jog	XT or 55-65 min	60-70 min	FFLR: 14-16 miles w/ the last 2-4 miles @ goal HM pace
8	Half Marathon	XT or 55-65 min	FR: 10-12 x 1 min w/ 1 min jog	60-70 min	TI: 3 x 2 miles w/ 5 min jog	XT or 55-65 min	60-70 min	LR: 14-18 miles
9	Half Marathon	XT or 55-65 min	PR: 80-90 min w/ last 20 minutes fast	60-70 min	SP: 5-6 x 1 mile w/ 800m jog	XT or 55-65 min	60-70 min	FFLR: 14-16 miles w/ the last 2-4 miles @ goal HM pace
10	Half Marathon	XT or 55-65 min	60-70 min	60-70 min	TR: 3-5 miles	XT or 55-65 min	60-70 min	LR: 105-120 min
11	Peak	XT or 55-65 min	FR: 10-12 x 1 min w/ 1 min jog	40-50 min	SS: 6 miles	XT or 50 min	40-50 min	FFLR: 12-14 miles w/ the last 2-4 miles @ goal HM pace
12	Peak	XT or 55-65 min	CI: 4-5 x 1000m w/ 200m	30-40 min	FR: 8-10 x 1 min w/ 1 min jog	XT or 30 min	30-40 min	RACE: Half Marathon

KEY: min = minutes
km = kilometers
LR = Long Run (p. 100)
PR = Progression Run (p. 220)
SP = Speed Workout (p. 129)
LS = Leg Speed (p. 142)

Mi = miles
OFF = No exercise
FR = Fartlek Run (p. 131)
TI = Tempo Intervals (p. 115)
SS = Steady State Run (p. 112)
Hills = Hill Workout (p. 217)

m = meters
XT = cross-training
CI = Cruise Intervals (p. 117)
FFLR = Fast Finish Long Run (p. 211)
TR = Tempo Run (p. 114)

MCMILLAN RUNNING

McMillan **MARATHON** Training Plan: **2-3 DAYS** of running per week

WEEK	PHASE	1	2	3	4	5	6	7
1	Prep-Speed	OFF	30-45 min	XT or 30-45 min	FR: 8-10 x 1 min on 1 min off	OFF or XT	XT or 30-45 min	LR: 8-10 miles
2	Prep-Speed	OFF	30-45 min	XT or 30-45 min	FR: 3-4 x 2 min on 1 min off	OFF or XT	XT or 30-45 min	LR: 8-10 miles
3	Mara	OFF	45-60 min	XT or 30-45 min	CI: 4-6 x 800m w/ 200m jog	OFF or XT	XT or 30-45 min	LR: 10-12 miles
4	Mara	OFF	80-100 min	XT or 30-45 min	PR: 50-60 min w/ last 20 min fast	OFF or XT	XT or 30-45 min	90 min 3rds PR
5	Mara	OFF	60-75 min	XT or 30-45 min	Yasso 800s: 6-8 x 800m	OFF or XT	XT or 30-45 min	LR: 14-16 miles
6	Mara	OFF	80-100 min	XT or 30-45 min	TR: 2-4 miles	OFF or XT	XT or 30-45 min	LR: 16-18 miles
7	Mara	OFF	70-85 min	XT or 30-45 min	TI: 3 x 2 miles w/ 4 min jog	OFF or XT	XT or 30-45 min	90 min 3rds PR
8	Mara	OFF	80-100 min	XT or 30-45 min	Yasso 800s: 8-10 x 800m	OFF or XT	XT or 30-45 min	FFLR: 14-18 miles w/ last 6-8 miles at marathon GP or slightly faster
9	Mara	OFF	70-85 min	XT or 30-45 min	TR: 3-5 miles	OFF or XT	XT or 30-45 min	LR: 18-22 miles
10	Mara	OFF	80-100 min	XT or 30-45 min	PR: 50-60 min w/ last 20 min fast	OFF or XT	XT or 30-45 min	90 min 3rds PR
11	Peak	OFF	40 min	XT or 30-45 min	TI: 3 x 2000m w/ 400m jog	OFF or XT	XT or 40 min	FFLR: 12m w/ last 6 miles at marathon GP or slightly faster
12	Peak	OFF	30-40 min	CI: 4-5 x 1000m w/ 200m jog	45 min	OFF or XT	XT or 30 min	RACE: Marathon

KEY: min = minutes
km = kilometers
LR = Long Run (p. 100)
PR = Progression Run (p. 220)
SP = Speed Workout (p. 129)
LS = Leg Speed (p. 142)

Mi = miles
OFF = No exercise
FR = Fartlek Run (p. 131)
TI = Tempo Intervals (p. 115)
TR = Tempo Run (p. 114)
GP = Goal Pace (p. 214)

m = meters
XT = cross-training
CI = Cruise Intervals (p. 117)
FFLR = Fast Finish Long Run (p. 211)
Yasso 800s (p. 212)

MCMILLAN RUNNING

McMillan **MARATHON** Training Plan: **4-5 DAYS** of running per week

WEEK	PHASE	1	2	3	4	5	6	7
1	Prep-Speed	OFF or XT	PR: 70-80 min w/ last 20-30 min fast	55-65 min	FR: 10-12 x 1 min w/ 1 min jog	OFF or 30-45 min	XT or 55-65 min	LR: 14-16 miles
2	Prep-Speed	OFF or XT	LS: 8-10 x 25 sec w/ 1 min jog	55-65 min	FR: 5 x 2 min on 1 min off	OFF or 30-45 min	XT or 55-65 min	LR: 16-18 miles
3	Mara	OFF or XT	80-90 min	55-65 min	CI: 6-8 x 1000m w/ 200m jog	OFF or 30-45 min	XT or 55-65 min	90 min 3rds PR
4	Mara	OFF or XT	FR: 12-15 x 1 min w/ 1 min jog	55-65 min	TI: 4-5 x 2000m w/ 400m jog	OFF or 30-45 min	XT or 60-75 min	LR: 16-20 miles
5	Mara	OFF or XT	90-105 min	55-65 min	Yasso 800s: 6-8 x 800m	OFF or 30-45 min	XT or 60-75 min	LR: 18-22 miles
6	Mara	OFF or XT	FR: 12-15 x 1 min w/ 1 min	55-65 min	TR: 3-5 miles	OFF or 30-45 min	XT or 60-75 min	FFLR: 16-20m w/ last 6-8 miles at marathon GP
7	Mara	OFF or XT	90-105 min	55-65 min	TI: 3 x 2 miles w/ 4 min jog	OFF or 30-45 min	XT or 60-75 min	LR: 18-22 miles
8	Mara	OFF or XT	FR: 12-15 x 1 min w/ 1 min jog	55-65 min	Yasso 800s: 8-10 x 800m	OFF or 30-45 min	XT or 60-75 min	FFLR: 14-18 miles w/ last 6-8 miles at marathon GP
9	Mara	OFF or XT	90-105 min	55-65 min	TR: 5-7 miles	OFF or 30-45 min	XT or 60-75 min	LR: 20-24 miles
10	Mara	OFF or XT	FR: 12-15 x 1 min w/ 1 min jog	55-65 min	FR: 6-8 x 2 min w/ 1 min jog	OFF or 30-45 min	XT or 60-75 min	FFLR: 14-18 miles w/ last 6-8 miles at marathon GP
11	Peak	OFF or XT	FR: 8-10 x 1 min w/ 1 min jog	40 min	TI: 3 x 2000m w/ 400m jog	OFF or 30-45 min	XT or 50 min	FFLR: 12 miles w/ last 6 miles at marathon GP
12	Peak	OFF or XT	LS: 8-10 x 25 sec w/ 1 min jog	CI: 4-5 x 1000m w/ 200m jog	45 min	OFF or 30-45 min	XT or 30 min	RACE: Marathon

KEY: min = minutes
km = kilometers
LR = Long Run (p. 100)
PR = Progression Run (p. 220)
SP = Speed Workout (p. 129)
LS = Leg Speed (p. 142)

Mi = miles
OFF = No exercise
FR = Fartlek Run (p. 131)
TI = Tempo Intervals (p. 115)
TR = Tempo Run (p. 114)
GP = Goal Pace (p. 214)

m = meters
XT = cross-training
CI = Cruise Intervals (p. 117)
FFLR = Fast Finish Long Run (p. 211)
Yasso 800s (p. 212)

MCMILLAN RUNNING

McMillan **MARATHON** Training Plan: **6-7 DAYS** of running per week

WEEK	PHASE	1	2	3	4	5	6	7
1	Prep - Speed	XT or 55-65 min	PR: 70-80 min w/ 20 min fast	60-75 min	SP: 12-16 x 400m w/ 200m jog	60-75 min	XT or 55-65 min	LR: 16-20 Mi
2	Prep - Speed	XT or 55-65 min	FR: 12-15 x 1 min w/ 1 min jog	60-75 min	SP: 6-8 x 800m w/ 400m jog	60-75 min	XT or 55-65 min	LR: 16-20 Mi
3	Mara	XT or 55-65 min	80-90 min	60-75 min	CI: 8-10 x 1000m w/ 200m jog	60-75 min	XT or 55-65 min	90 min 3rds PR
4	Mara	XT or 30-40 min	FR: 12-15 x 1 min w/ 1 min jog	40-50 min	TI: 4-5 x 2000m w/ 400m jog	40-50 min	XT or 30-40 min	LR: 18-22 Mi
5	Mara	XT or 55-65 min	90-105 min	60-75 min	Yasso 800s: 8-10 x 800m	60-75 min	XT or 60-75 min	LR: 20-24 Mi
6	Mara	XT or 55-65 min	FR: 12-15 x 1 min w/ 1 min jog	60-75 min	TR: 3-5 miles	60-75 min	XT or 60-75 min	FFLR: 16-20 Mi w/ last 6-8 Mi fast
7	Mara	XT or 55-65 min	90-105 min	60-75 min	TI: 3-4 x 2 miles w/ 4 min jog	60-75 min	XT or 60-75 min	LR: 22-26 Mi
8	Mara	XT or 30-40 min	FR: 12-15 x 1 min w/ 1 min jog	40-50 min	Yasso 800s: 8-10 x 800m	40-50 min	XT or 30-40 min	FFLR: 16-20 Mi w/ last 6-8 Mi fast
9	Mara	XT or 55-65 min	90-105 min	60-75 min	TR: 5-7 miles	60-75 min	XT or 60-75 min	LR: 22-28 Mi
10	Mara	XT or 55-65 min	FR: 12-15 x 1 min w/ 1 min jog	60-75 min	GP: 7-10 miles at marathon goal pace	60-75 min	XT or 60-75 min	FFLR: 14-18 Mi w/ last 6-8 Mi fast
11	Peak	XT or 50 min	FR: 8-10 x 1 min w/ 1 min jog	40 min	TI: 3 x 2000m w/ 400m jog	40 min	XT or 50 min	FFLR: 12 Mi w/ last 6 Mi fast
12	Peak	XT or 30 min	LS: 8-10 x 25 sec w/ 1 min jog	CI: 4-5 x 1000m w/ 200m jog	45 min	40 min	XT or 30 min	RACE: Marathon

KEY: min = minutes
km = kilometers
LR = Long Run (p. 100)
PR = Progression Run (p. 220)
SP = Speed Workout (p.129)
LS = Leg Speed (p. 142)

Mi = miles
OFF = No exercise
FR = Fartlek Run (p. 131)
TI = Tempo Intervals (p. 115)
TR = Tempo Run (p. 114)
GP = Goal Pace (p. 214)

m = meters
XT = cross-training
CI = Cruise Intervals (p.117)
FFLR = Fast Finish Long Run (p. 211)
Yasso 800s (p. 212)

Glossary

"Runner speak" can be subjective and confusing, so here's a cheat sheet of some common terms:

BQ

Short for "Boston Qualifying Time."

Cruise Intervals

Cruise intervals improve your lactate threshold (as do *tempo runs* and *tempo intervals*). Cruise intervals are run at a medium-hard effort and include short recovery intervals in between. Breathing is fast and on the verge of out-of-control, and the focus is more on your running rhythm than on pushing hard.

Down Week

A week where you reduce your training load (i.e., mileage) by 15–25% to allow the musculoskeletal system and the mind to recover and rejuvenate for the next training segment.

Easy Run

Easy runs make up the bulk of a runner's training plan. The run is at an easy effort, and breathing is always under control so that you can carry on a conversation with your training partners. There should be no lasting fatigue from an easy run.

Fartlek Run

Fartlek is a Scandinavian word meaning "speed play." Often called a "pace-change workout," a fartlek run involves periods of faster running alternating with slower running. Typically, fartlek runs are run at 5K–10K effort where you get slightly out of breath during the "on" (fast running) part and then regain your breath on the "off" (recovery-pace) part.

Fast Finish Long Run

Unlike a long run where the pace is mostly consistent, a fast finish long run is a long run where you run very fast at the end, sort of like a longer *progression run*. Fast finish long runs are a key to racing well at the half-marathon and marathon distances.

Goal-Pace Run

Dialing in goal pace is critical for race success. Goal-pace runs simply involve running at your goal race pace. As the race nears, feeling comfortable at your goal pace is another indicator that you are race ready.

Hill Repeats

Hill repeats involve repetitions of sprinting uphill and jogging downhill to recover. They are an efficient way to build leg strength, speed, and aerobic capacity.

Hitting the Wall

Also called "bonking," hitting the wall is the point in the race when your muscle glycogen stores become depleted and you feel like you are hit by a "wall" of fatigue.

Long Run

Long runs are similar to *easy runs,* but they last much longer. The effort is still easy, but it may become more difficult due to the duration (as opposed to the intensity) of the run. There may be some lasting fatigue from a long run, so extra recovery is often required after.

PR

"Personal record," or the fastest time you have ever run for a given distance; also sometimes called "PB" or "personal best."

Progression Run

As the name suggests, a progression run starts at one pace and gets faster toward the end of the run. Progression runs can vary but often include the last 5–20 minutes at a medium-hard to hard running pace, which closely mimics the increased effort experienced across races.

Rest Day

Training stresses the body. To grow stronger and fitter, there must be recovery. Rest days are used to enhance recovery and may be a complete day of rest or cross-training.

Running Economy

Running economy refers to how much oxygen you use when you run at a given pace. The less you use, the better your running economy.

Speed Workout

A speed workout challenges your mental and physical fortitude. The effort is hard to very hard, and the pace is 5K race pace or faster. Recovery intervals are taken between the fast running repeats to allow you to catch your breath. The last few repeats will likely feel very hard, but that helps prepare you for the challenge at the end of your race.

Strides

Strides are short, fast, but controlled runs of 50–150 meters. They are used both to build speed and efficiency in training and to warm up before a race.

Tempo Intervals

Tempo intervals are broken-up *tempo runs*. They usually last 5–20 minutes and include short recovery intervals in between. Effort may start at medium on the first few repeats and build to medium-hard by the last few repeats.

Tempo Run

The tempo run is a medium-effort run that improves your lactate threshold (the point where lactic acid begins to build up). Tempo runs usually last 10–40 minutes and breathing is fast but under control. Training partners can usually speak in short sentences during a tempo run. Running too fast is a common error, so remember to keep a tempo run at a medium effort and never lose your breath.

Taper

Tapering involves cutting back mileage and workout intensity one day to three weeks before a big race (depending on race distance). Tapering allows your body to rest so that it is ready for peak performance on race day.

ACKNOWLEDGEMENTS

The path to this book has been paved with support. The sport of running has given our lives purpose and passion. Coaches, teachers, teammates, and training partners have offered (and continue to offer) guidance, support, and inspiration. Mentors and family members continually pass down knowledge, encouragement, and love. And finally, athletes from around the world—some just coming off the couch, others chasing PRs and Boston qualifying times, and a few going for the gold—all have been instrumental in helping us help them. This book is dedicated to each and every one of you.

Special thanks to everyone who encouraged us to put these thoughts onto paper, who helped proof the manuscript, who posed for photos, who contributed their expertise, who offered feedback, and who otherwise shaped what you now hold in your hands. Thank you.

Printed in Great Britain
by Amazon

81508853R10193